on
Provence

Published by Hesperus Press Limited
28 Mortimer Street, London W1W 7RD
www.hesperuspress.com

Selection taken from *A Little Tour in France*, first published 1884
First published by Hesperus Press Limited, 2014

Designed and typeset by Fraser Muggeridge studio
Printed and bound by CPI Group (UK) Ltd, Croydon, CR0 4YY

ISBN: 978-1-84391-625-3

James
on
Provence

'on'

Prologue

We good Americans – I say it without presumption – are too apt to think that France is Paris, just as we are accused of being too apt to think that Paris is the celestial city. This is by no means the case, fortunately for those persons who take an interest in modern Gaul, and yet are still left vaguely unsatisfied by that epitome of civilization which stretches from the Arc de Triomphe to the Gymnase theatre. It had already been intimated to the author of these light pages that there are many good things in the *doux pays de France* of which you get no hint in a walk between those ornaments of the capital; but the truth had been revealed only in quick-flashing glimpses, and he was conscious of a desire to look it well in the face. To this end he started, one rainy morning in mid-September, for the charming little city of Tours, from which point it seemed possible to make a variety of fruitful excursions. His excursions resolved themselves ultimately into a journey through several provinces – a journey which had its dull moments (as one may defy any journey not to have), but which enabled him to feel that his proposition was demonstrated. France may be Paris, but Paris is not France; that was perfectly evident on the return to the capital.

I must not speak, however, as if I had discovered the provinces. They were discovered, or at least revealed by Balzac, if by anyone, and are now easily accessible to visitors. It is true, I met no visitors, or only one or two, whom it was pleasant to meet. Throughout my little tour I was almost the only tourist. That is perhaps one reason why it was so successful.

I

At Narbonne I took up my abode at the house of a *serrurier mécanicien*, and was very thankful for the accommodation. It was my misfortune to arrive at this ancient city late at night, on the eve of market day; and market day at Narbonne is a very serious affair. The inns, on this occasion, are stuffed with wine-dealers; for the country roundabout, dedicated almost exclusively to Bacchus, has hitherto escaped the phylloxera. This deadly enemy of the grape is encamped over the Midi in a hundred places; blighted vineyards and ruined proprietors being quite the order of the day. The signs of distress are more frequent as you advance into Provence, many of the vines being laid under water, in the hope of washing the plague away. There are healthy regions still, however, and the vintners find plenty to do at Narbonne. The traffic in wine appeared to be the sole thought of the Narbonnais; everyone I spoke to had something to say about the harvest of gold that bloomed under its influence. 'C'est inouï, Monsieur, l'argent qu'il y a dans ce pays. Des gens a qui la vente de leur vin rapporte jusqu'à 500,000 francs par an.' That little speech, addressed to me by a gentleman at the inn, gives the note of these revelations. It must be said that there was little in the appearance either of the town or of its population to suggest the possession of such treasures. Narbonne is a *sale petite ville* in all the force of the term, and my first impression on arriving there was an extreme regret that I had not remained for the night at the lovely Carcassonne. My journey from that delectable spot lasted a couple of hours, and was performed in darkness, a darkness not so dense, however, but that I was able to make out, as we passed it, the great figure of Béziers, whose ancient roofs and towers, clustered on a goodly hilltop, looked as fantastic as you please. I know not what appearance Béziers may present by day; but by night it has quite the grand air.

On issuing from the station at Narbonne, I found that the only vehicle in waiting was a kind of bastard tramcar, a thing shaped as if it had been meant to go upon rails; that is, equipped with small wheels, placed beneath it, and with a platform at either end, but destined to rattle over the stones like the most vulgar of omnibuses. To complete the oddity of this conveyance, it was under the supervision, not of a conductor, but of a conductress. A fair young woman, with a pouch suspended from her girdle, had command of the platform; and as soon as the car was full she jolted us into the town through clouds of the thickest dust I ever have swallowed. I have had occasion to speak of the activity of women in France, of the way they are always in the ascendant; and here was a signal example of their general utility. The young lady I have mentioned conveyed her whole company to the wretched little Hôtel de France, where it is to be hoped that some of them found a lodging. For myself, I was informed that the place was crowded from cellar to attic, and that its inmates were sleeping three or four in a room. At Carcassonne I should have had a bad bed, but at Narbonne, apparently, I was to have no bed at all. I passed an hour or two of flat suspense, while fate settled the question of whether I should go on to Perpignan, return to Béziers, or still discover a modest couch at Narbonne. I shall not have suffered in vain, however, if my example serves to deter other travellers from alighting unannounced at that city on a Wednesday evening. The retreat to Béziers, not attempted in time, proved impossible, and I was assured that at Perpignan, which I should not reach till midnight, the affluence of wine-dealers was not less than at Narbonne. I interviewed every hostess in the town, and got no satisfaction but distracted shrugs. Finally, at an advanced hour, one of the servants of the Hôtel de France, where I had attempted to dine, came to me in triumph to proclaim that he had secured for me a charming apartment in a *maison bourgeoise*. I took possession of it gratefully, in spite of its having an entrance like a stable, and being pervaded by an odor compared with which that of a stable would have been delicious. As I have mentioned, my landlord was a locksmith, and he had strange machines which rumbled and whirred in the rooms below my own. Nevertheless, I slept, and I dreamed of Carcassonne. It was better to do that than to dream of the Hôtel de France.

I was obliged to cultivate relations with the cuisine of this establishment. Nothing could have been more *meridional*; indeed, both the dirty little inn and Narbonne at large seemed to me to have the infirmities of the south, without its usual graces. Narrow, noisy, shabby, belittered and encumbered, filled with clatter and chatter, the Hôtel de France would have been described in perfection by Alphonse Daudet. For what struck me above all in it was the note of the Midi, as he has represented it – the sound of universal talk. The landlord sat at supper with sundry friends, in a kind of glass cage, with a genial indifference to arriving guests; the waiters tumbled over the loose luggage in the hall; the travellers who had been turned away leaned gloomily against doorposts; and the landlady, surrounded by confusion, unconscious of responsibility, and animated only by the spirit of conversation, bandied high-voiced compliments with the *voyageurs de commerce*. At ten o'clock in the morning there was a table d'hôte for breakfast, a wonderful repast, which overflowed into every room and pervaded the whole establishment. I sat down with a hundred hungry marketers, fat, brown, greasy men, with a good deal of the rich soil of Languedoc adhering to their hands and their boots. I mention the latter articles because they almost put them on the table. It was very hot, and there were swarms of flies; the viands had the strongest odor; there was in particular a horrible mixture known as *gras-double*, a light gray, glutinous, nauseating mess, which my companions devoured in large quantities. A man opposite to me had the dirtiest fingers I ever saw; a collection of fingers which in England would have excluded him from a farmers' ordinary. The conversation was mainly bucolic; though a part of it, I remember, at the table at which I sat, consisted of a discussion as to whether or not the maid-servant were *sage* – a discussion which went on under the nose of this young lady, as she carried about the dreadful *gras-double*, and to which she contributed the most convincing blushes. It was thoroughly *meridional*.

In going to Narbonne I had of course counted upon Roman remains; but when I went forth in search of them I perceived that I had hoped too fondly. There is really nothing in the place to speak of; that is, on the day of my visit there was nothing but the market, which was in complete possession. 'This intricate, curious, but lifeless town,' Murray calls it; yet to me it appeared overflowing with life. Its streets are mere crooked, dirty lanes, bordered with perfectly insignificant houses; but they were filled with the same clatter and chatter that I had found at the hotel. The market was held partly in the little square of the hôtel de ville, a structure which a flattering woodcut in the Guide Joanne had given me a desire to behold. The reality was not impressive, the old color of the front having been completely restored away. Such interest as it superficially possesses it derives from a fine mediaeval tower which rises beside it, with turrets at the angles, always a picturesque thing. The rest of the market was held in another *place*, still shabbier than the first, which lies beyond the canal. The Canal du Midi flows through the town, and, spanned at this point by a small suspension-bridge, presented a certain sketchability. On the further side were the venders and chaf-ferers, old women under awnings and big umbrellas, rickety tables piled high with fruit, white caps and brown faces, blouses, sabots, donkeys. Beneath this picture was another – a long row of washerwomen, on their knees on the edge of the canal, pounding and wringing the dirty linen of Narbonne – no great quantity, to judge by the costume of the people. Innumerable rusty men, scattered all over the place, were buying and selling wine, strad-dling about in pairs, in groups, with their hands in their pockets, and packed together at the doors of the cafes. They were mostly fat and brown and unshaven; they ground their teeth as they talked; they were very *meridionaux*.

The only two lions at Narbonne are the cathedral and the museum, the latter of which is quartered in the *hôtel de ville*. The cathedral, closely shut in by houses, and with the west front undergoing repairs, is singular in two respects. It consists exclusively of a choir, which is of the end of the thirteenth century and the beginning of the next, and of great magnificence. There is absolutely nothing else. This choir, of extraordinary elevation, forms the whole church. I sat there a good while; there was no other visitor. I had taken a great dislike to poor little Narbonne, which struck me as sordid and overheated, and this place seemed to extend to me, as in the Middle Ages, the privilege of sanctuary. It is a very solemn corner. The other peculiarity of the cathedral is that, externally, it bristles with battlements, having anciently formed part of the defences of the *archevêché*, which is beside it and which connects it with the *hôtel de ville*. This combination of the church and the fortress is very curious, and during the Middle Ages was not without its value. The palace of the former archbishops of Narbonne (the *hôtel de ville* of today forms part of it) was both an asylum and an arsenal during the hideous wars by which the Languedoc was ravaged in the thirteenth century. The whole mass of buildings is jammed together in a manner that from certain points of view makes it far from apparent which feature is which. The museum occupies several chambers at the top of the *hôtel de ville*, and is not an imposing collection. It was closed, but I induced the portress to let me in – a silent, cadaverous person, in a black coif, like a *Beguine*, who sat knitting in one of the windows while I went the rounds. The number of Roman fragments is small, and their quality is not the finest; I must add that this impression was hastily gathered. There is indeed a work of art in one of the rooms which creates a presumption in favor of the place – the portrait (rather a good one) of a citizen of Narbonne, whose name I forget, who is described as having devoted all his time and his intelligence to collecting the objects by which the visitor is surrounded. This excellent man was a connoisseur, and the visitor is doubtless often an ignoramus.

II

Cette, with its glistening houses white,
   Curves with the curving beach away
To where the lighthouse beacons bright,
   Far in the bay.

That stanza of Matthew Arnold's, which I happened to remember, gave a certain importance to the half-hour I spent in
the buffet of the station at Cette while I waited for the train to
Montpellier. I had left Narbonne in the afternoon, and by the
time I reached Cette the darkness had descended. I therefore
missed the sight of the glistening houses, and had to console
myself with that of the beacon in the bay, as well as with
a *bouillon* of which I partook at the buffet aforesaid; for, since
the morning, I had not ventured to return to the table d'hôte at
Narbonne. The Hôtel Nevet, at Montpellier, which I reached an
hour later, has an ancient renown all over the south of France,
advertises itself, I believe, as *le plus vaste du midi*. It seemed to
me the model of a good provincial inn; a big rambling, creaking
establishment, with brown, labyrinthine corridors, a queer old
open-air vestibule, into which the diligence, in the *bon temps*,
used to penetrate, and an hospitality more expressive than that of
the new caravansaries. It dates from the days when Montpellier
was still accounted a fine winter residence for people with weak
lungs; and this rather melancholy tradition, together with the
former celebrity of the school of medicine still existing there,
but from which the glory has departed, helps to account for its
combination of high antiquity and vast proportions. The old
hotels were usually more concentrated; but the school of medicine passed for one of the attractions of Montpellier. Long
before Mentone was discovered or Colorado invented, British
invalids travelled down through France in the post-chaise or the
public coach to spend their winters in the wonderful place which

boasted both a climate and a faculty. The air is mild, no doubt, but there are refinements of mildness which were not then suspected, and which in a more analytic age have carried the annual wave far beyond Montpellier. The place is charming, all the same; and it served the purpose of John Locke, who made a long stay there, between 1675 and 1679, and became acquainted with a noble fellow-visitor, Lord Pembroke, to whom he dedicated the famous Essay. There are places that please, without your being able to say wherefore, and Montpellier is one of the number. It has some charming views, from the great promenade of the Peyrou; but its position is not strikingly fair. Beyond this it contains a good museum and the long facades of its school, but these are its only definite treasures. Its cathedral struck me as quite the weakest I had seen, and I remember no other monument that made up for it. The place has neither the gayety of a modern nor the solemnity of an ancient town, and it is agreeable as certain women are agreeable who are neither beautiful nor clever. An Italian would remark that it is sympathetic; a German would admit that it is gemuthlich. I spent two days there, mostly in the rain, and even under these circumstances I carried away a kindly impression. I think the Hôtel Nevet had something to do with it, and the sentiment of relief with which, in a quiet, even a luxurious, room that looked out on a garden, I reflected that I had washed my hands of Narbonne. The phylloxera has destroyed the vines in the country that surrounds Montpellier, and at that moment I was capable of rejoicing in the thought that I should not breakfast with vintners.

The gem of the place is the Musée Fabre, one of the best collections of paintings in a provincial city. Francois Fabre, a native of Montpellier, died there in 1837, after having spent a considerable part of his life in Italy, where he had collected a good many valuable pictures and some very poor ones, the latter class including several from his own hand. He was the hero of a remarkable episode, having succeeded no less a person than Vittorio Alfieri in the affections of no less a person than Louise de Stolberg, Countess of Albany, widow of no less a person than Charles Edward Stuart, the second pretender to the British crown. Surely no woman ever was associated sentimentally with three figures more diverse – a disqualified sovereign, an Italian dramatist, and a bad French painter. The productions of M. Fabre, who followed in the steps of David, bear the stamp of a cold mediocrity; there is not much to be said even for the portrait of the genial countess (her life has been written by M. Saint-René-Taillandier, who depicts her as delightful), which hangs in Florence, in the gallery of the Uffizzi, and makes a pendant to a likeness of Alfieri by the same author. Stendhal, in his *Memoires d'un Touriste*, says that this work of art represents her as a cook who has pretty hands. I am delighted to have an opportunity of quoting Stendhal, whose two volumes of the *Memoires d'un Touriste* every traveller in France should carry in his portmanteau. I have had this opportunity more than once, for I have met him at 'Tours, at Nantes, at Bourges; and everywhere he is suggestive. But he has the defect that he is never pictorial, that he never by any chance makes an image, and that his style is perversely colorless, for a man so fond of contemplation. His taste is often singularly false; it is the taste of the early years of the present century, the period that produced clocks surmounted with sentimental 'subjects'. Stendhal does not admire these clocks, but he almost does. He admires Domenichino and Guercino, and prizes the Bolognese school of painters because they 'spoke to the soul'. He is a votary of the new classic, is fond of tall, squire, regular buildings, and thinks Nantes, for instance, full of the 'air noble'. It was a pleasure to me to reflect that five-and-forty years ago he had alighted in that city, at the very inn in which I spent a night, and which looks down on the Place Graslin and the theatre. The hotel that was the best in 1837 appears to be the best today. On the subject of Touraine, Stendhal is extremely refreshing; he finds the scenery meagre and much overrated, and proclaims his opinion with perfect frankness. He does, however, scant justice to the banks of the Loire; his want of appreciation of the picturesque – want of the sketcher's sense – causes him to miss half the charm of a landscape which is nothing if not 'quiet', as a painter would say, and of which the felicities reveal themselves only to waiting eyes. He even despises the Indre, the river of Madame Sand. The *Memoires d'un Touriste* are written in the character of a commercial traveller, and the author has nothing to say about Chenonceaux or Chambord, or indeed about any of the chateaux of that part of France; his system being to talk only of the large towns, where he may be supposed to find a market for his goods. It was his ambition to pass for an ironmonger. But in the large towns he is usually excellent company, though as discursive as Sterne, and strangely indifferent, for a man of imagination, to those superficial aspects of things which the poor pages now before the reader are mainly an attempt to render. It is his conviction that Alfieri, at Florence, bored the Countess of Albany terribly; and he adds that the famous Gallophobe died of jealousy of the little painter from Montpellier. The Countess of Albany left her property to Fabre; and I suppose some of the pieces in the museum of his native town used to hang in the sunny saloons of that fine old palace on the Arno which is still pointed out to the stranger in Florence as the residence of Alfieri.

The institution has had other benefactors, notably a certain M. Bruyas, who has enriched it with an extraordinary number of portraits of himself. As these, however, are by different hands, some of them distinguished, we may suppose that it was less the model than the artists to whom M. Bruyas wished to give publicity. Easily first are two large specimens of David Teniers, which are incomparable for brilliancy and a glowing perfection of execution. I have a weakness for this singular genius, who combined the delicate with the grovelling, and I have rarely seen richer examples. Scarcely less valuable is a Gerard Dow which hangs near them, though it must rank lower as having kept less of its freshness. This Gerard Dow did me good; for a master is a master, whatever he may paint. It represents a woman paring carrots, while a boy before her exhibits a mousetrap in which he has caught a frightened victim. The good-wife has spread a cloth on the top of a big barrel which serves her as a table, and on this brown, greasy napkin, of which the texture is wonderfully rendered, lie the raw vegetables she is preparing for domestic consumption. Beside the barrel is a large caldron lined with copper, with a rim of brass. The way these things are painted brings tears to the eyes; but they give the measure of the Musée Fabre, where two specimens of Teniers and a Gerard Dow are the jewels. The Italian pictures are of small value; but there is a work by Sir Joshua Reynolds, said to be the only one in France – an infant Samuel in prayer, apparently a repetition of the picture in England which inspired the little plaster image, disseminated in Protestant lands, that we used to admire in our childhood. Sir Joshua, somehow, was an eminently Protestant painter; no one can forget that, who in the National Gallery in London has looked at the picture in which he represents several young ladies as nymphs, voluminously draped, hanging garlands over a statue – a picture suffused indefinably with the Anglican spirit, and exasperating to a member of one of the Latin races. It is an odd chance, therefore, that has led him into that part of France where Protestants have been least *bien vus*. This is the country of the dragonnades of Louis XIV and of the pastors of the desert. From the garden of the Peyrou, at Montpellier, you may see the hills of the Cévennes, to which they of the religion fled for safety, and out of which they were hunted and harried.

I have only to add, in regard to the Musée Fabre, that it contains the portrait of its founder – a little, pursy, fat-faced, elderly man, whose countenance contains few indications of the power that makes distinguished victims. He is, however, just such a personage as the mind's eye sees walking on the terrace of the Peyrou of an October afternoon in the early years of the century; a plump figure in a chocolate-colored coat and a *culotte* that exhibits a good leg – a culotte provided with a watch-fob from which a heavy seal is suspended. This Peyrou (to come to it at last) is a wonderful place, especially to be found in a little provincial city. France is certainly the country of towns that aim at completeness; more than in other lands, they contain stately features as a matter of course. We should never have ceased to hear about the Peyrou, if fortune had placed it at a Shrewsbury or a Buffalo. It is true that the place enjoys a certain celebrity at home, which it amply deserves, moreover; for nothing could be more impressive and monumental. It consists of an 'elevated platform', as Murray says – an immense terrace, laid out, in the highest part of the town, as a garden, and commanding in all directions a view which in clear weather must be of the finest. I strolled there in the intervals of showers, and saw only the nearer beauties – a great pompous arch of triumph in honor of Louis XIV (which is not, properly speaking, in the garden, but faces it, straddling across the *place* by which you approach it from the town), an equestrian statue of that monarch set aloft in the middle of the terrace, and a very exalted and complicated fountain, which forms a background to the picture. This fountain gushes from a kind of hydraulic temple, or *chateau d'eau*, to which you ascend by broad flights of steps, and which is fed by a splendid aqueduct, stretched in the most ornamental and unexpected manner across the neighboring valley. All this work dates from the middle of the last century. The combination of features – the triumphal arch, or gate; the wide, fair terrace, with its beautiful view; the statue of the grand monarch; the big architectural fountain, which would not surprise one at Rome, but does surprise one at Montpellier; and to complete the effect, the extraordinary aqueduct, charmingly foreshortened – all this is worthy of a capital, of a little court-city. The whole place, with its repeated steps, its balustrades, its massive and plentiful stonework, is full of the air of the last century – *sent bien son dix-huitième siècle*; none the less so, I am afraid, that, as I read in my faithful Murray, after the revocation of the Edict of Nantes, the block, the stake, the wheel, had been erected here for the benefit of the desperate Camisards.

III

It was a pleasure to feel oneself in Provence again – the land where the silver-gray earth is impregnated with the light of the sky. To celebrate the event, as soon as I arrived at Nîmes I engaged a caleche to convey me to the Pont du Gard. The day was yet young, and it was perfectly fair; it appeared well, for a longish drive, to take advantage, without delay, of such security. After I had left the town I became more intimate with that Provençal charm which I had already enjoyed from the window of the train, and which glowed in the sweet sunshine and the white rocks, and lurked in the smoke-puffs of the little olives. The olive trees in Provence are half the landscape. They are neither so tall, so stout, nor so richly contorted as I have seen them beyond the Alps; but this mild colorless bloom seems the very texture of the country. The road from Nîmes, for a distance of fifteen miles, is superb; broad enough for an army, and as white and firm as a dinner-table. It stretches away over undulations which suggest a kind of harmony; and in the curves it makes through the wide, free country, where there is never a hedge or a wall, and the detail is always exquisite, there is something majestic, almost processional. Some twenty minutes before I reached the little inn that marks the termination of the drive, my vehicle met with an accident which just missed being serious, and which engaged the attention of a gentleman, who, followed by his groom and mounted on a strikingly handsome horse happened to ride up at the moment. This young man, who, with his good looks and charming manner, might have stepped out of a novel of Octave Feuillet, gave me some very intelligent advice in reference to one of my horses that had been injured, and was so good as to accompany me to the inn, with the resources of which he was acquainted, to see that his recommendations were carried out. The result of our interview was that he invited me to come and look at a small but ancient chateau in the neighborhood, which he had the happiness – not the greatest in the world, he intimated – to inhabit, and at which I engaged to present myself after I should have spent an hour at the Pont du Gard. For the moment, when we separated, I gave all my attention to that great structure. You are very near it before you see it; the ravine it spans suddenly opens and exhibits the picture. The scene at this point grows extremely beautiful. The ravine is the valley of the Gardon, which the road from Nîmes has followed some time without taking account of it, but which, exactly at the right distance from the aqueduct, deepens and expands, and puts on those characteristics which are best suited to give it effect. The gorge becomes romantic, still, and solitary, and, with its white rocks and wild shrubbery, hangs over the clear, colored river, in whose slow course there is here and there a deeper pool. Over the valley, from side to side, and ever so high in the air, stretch the three tiers of the tremendous bridge. They are unspeakably imposing, and nothing could well be more Roman. The hugeness, the solidity, the unexpectedness, the monumental rectitude of the whole thing leave you nothing to say – at the time – and make you stand gazing. You simply feel that it is noble and perfect, that it has the quality of greatness. A road, branching from the highway, descends to the level of the river and passes under one of the arches. This road has a wide margin of grass and loose stones, which slopes upward into the bank of the ravine. You may sit here as long as you please, staring up at the light, strong piers; the spot is extremely natural, though two or three stone benches have been erected on it. I remained there an hour and got a complete impression; the place was perfectly soundless, and for the time, at least, lonely; the splendid afternoon had begun to fade, and there was a fascination in the object I had come to see. It came to pass that at the same time I discovered in it a certain stupidity, a vague brutality. That element is rarely absent from great Roman work, which is wanting in the nice adaptation of the means to the end. The means are always exaggerated; the end is so much more than attained. The Roman rigidity was apt to overshoot the mark, and I suppose a race which could do nothing small is as defective as a race that can do nothing great. Of this Roman rigidity the Pont du Gard is an admirable example. It would be a great injustice, however, not to insist upon its beauty, a kind of manly beauty, that of an object constructed not to please but to serve, and impressive simply from the scale on which it carries out this intention. The number of arches in each tier is different; they are smaller and more numerous as they ascend. The preservation of the thing is extraordinary; nothing has crumbled or collapsed; every feature remains; and the huge blocks of stone, of a brownish-yellow, (as if they had been baked by the Provençal sun for eighteen centuries), pile themselves, without mortar or cement, as evenly as the day they were laid together. All this to carry the water of a couple of springs to a little provincial city! The conduit on the top has retained its shape and traces of the cement with which it was lined. When the vague twilight began to gather, the lonely valley seemed to fill itself with the shadow of the Roman name, as if the mighty empire were still as erect as the supports of the aqueduct; and it was open to a solitary tourist, sitting there sentimental, to believe that no people has ever been, or will ever be, as great as that, measured, as we measure the greatness of an individual, by the push they gave to what they undertook. The Pont du Gard is one of the three or four deepest impressions they have left; it speaks of them in a manner with which they might have been satisfied.

I feel as if it were scarcely discreet to indicate the whereabouts of the chateau of the obliging young man I had met on the way from Nîmes; I must content myself with saying that it nestled in an enchanting valley – *dans le fond*, as they say in France – and that I took my course thither on foot, after leaving the Pont du Gard. I find it noted in my journal as 'an adorable little corner'. The principal feature of the place is a couple of very ancient towers, brownish-yellow in hue, and mantled in scarlet Virginia creeper. One of these towers, reputed to be of Saracenic origin, is isolated, and is only the more effective; the other is incorporated in the house, which is delightfully fragmentary and irregular. It had got to be late by this time, and the lonely *castel* looked crepuscular and mysterious. An old housekeeper was sent for, who showed me the rambling interior; and then the young man took me into a dim old drawing room, which had no less than four chimney pieces, all unlighted, and gave me a refection of fruit and sweet wine. When I praised the wine and asked him what it was, he said simply, 'C'est du vin de ma mère!' Throughout my little journey I had never yet felt myself so far from Paris; and this was a sensation I enjoyed more than my host, who was an involuntary exile, consoling himself with laying out a *manège*, which he showed me as I walked away. His civility was great, and I was greatly touched by it. On my way back to the little inn where I had left my vehicle, I passed the Pont du Gard, and took another look at it. Its great arches made windows for the evening sky, and the rocky ravine, with its dusky cedars and shining river, was lonelier than before. At the inn I swallowed, or tried to swallow, a glass of horrible wine with my coachman; after which, with my reconstructed team, I drove back to Nîmes in the moonlight. It only added a more solitary whiteness to the constant sheen of the Provençal landscape.

IV

The weather the next day was equally fair, so that it seemed an imprudence not to make sure of Aigues-Mortes. Nîmes itself could wait; at a pinch, I could attend to Nîmes in the rain. It was my belief that Aigues-Mortes was a little gem, and it is natural to desire that gems should have an opportunity to sparkle. This is an excursion of but a few hours, and there is a little friendly, familiar, dawdling train that will convey you, in time for a noonday breakfast, to the small dead town where the blessed Saint-Louis twice embarked for the crusades. You may get back to Nîmes for dinner; the run – or rather the walk, for the train doesn't run – is of about an hour. I found the little journey charming, and looked out of the carriage window, on my right, at the distant Cévennes, covered with tones of amber and blue, and, all around, at vineyards red with the touch of October. The grapes were gone, but the plants had a color of their own. Within a certain distance of Aigues Mortes they give place to wide salt-marshes, traversed by two canals; and over this expanse the train rumbles slowly upon a narrow causeway, failing for some time, though you know you are near the object of your curiosity, to bring you to sight of anything but the horizon. Suddenly it appears, the towered and embattled mass, lying so low that the crest of its defences seems to rise straight out of the ground; and it is not till the train stops, close before them, that you are able to take the full measure of its walls.

Aigues-Mortes stands on the edge of a wide *étang*, or shallow inlet of the sea, the further side of which is divided by a narrow band of coast from the Gulf of Lyons. Next after Carcassonne, to which it forms an admirable *pendant*, it is the most perfect thing of the kind in France. It has a rival in the person of Avignon, but the ramparts of Avignon are much less effective. Like Carcassonne, it is completely surrounded with its old fortifications; and if they are far simpler in character (there is but one circle), they are quite as well preserved. The moat has been filled up, and the site of the town might be figured by a billiard-table without pockets. On this absolute level, covered with coarse grass, Aigues-Mortes presents quite the appearance of the walled town that a schoolboy draws upon his slate, or that we see in the background of early Flemish pictures – a simple parallelogram, of a contour almost absurdly bare, broken at intervals by angular towers and square holes. Such, literally speaking, is this delightful little city, which needs to be seen to tell its full story. It is extraordinarily pictorial, and if it is a very small sister of Carcassonne, it has at least the essential features of the family. Indeed, it is even more like an image and less like a reality than Carcassonne; for by position and prospect it seems even more detached from the life of the present day. It is true that Aigues-Mortes does a little business; it sees certain bags of salt piled into barges which stand in a canal beside it, and which carry their cargo into actual places. But nothing could well be more drowsy and desultory than this industry as I saw it prac-tised, with the aid of two or three brown peasants and under the eye of a solitary douanier, who strolled on the little quay beneath the western wall. 'C'est bien plaisant, c'est bien paisible,' said this worthy man, with whom I had some conversation; and pleasant and peaceful is the place indeed, though the former of these epithets may suggest an element of gayety in which Aigues-Mortes is deficient. The sand, the salt, the dull sea-view, surround it with a bright, quiet melancholy. There are fifteen towers and nine gates, five of which are on the southern side, overlooking the water. I walked all round the place three times (it doesn't take long), but lingered most under the southern wall, where the afternoon light slept in the dreamiest, sweetest way. I sat down on an old stone, and looked away to the desolate salt-marshes and the still, shining surface of the *étang*, and, as I did so, reflected that this was a queer little out-of-the-world corner to have been chosen, in the great dominions of either monarch, for that pompous interview which took place, in 1538, between Francis I and Charles V. It was also not easy to perceive how Louis IX, when in 1248 and 1270 he started for the Holy Land, set his army afloat in such very undeveloped channels. An hour later I purchased in the town a little pamphlet by M. Marius Topin, who undertakes to explain this latter anomaly, and to show that there is water enough in the port, as we may call it by courtesy, to have sustained a fleet of crusaders. I was unable to trace the channel that he points out, but was glad to believe that, as he contends, the sea has not retreated from the town since the thirteenth century. It was comfortable to think that things are not so changed as that. M. Topin indicates that the other French ports of the Mediterranean were not then *disponsibles*, and that Aigues-Mortes was the most eligible spot for an embarkation.

Behind the straight walls and the quiet gates the little town has not crumbled, like the Cité of Carcassonne. It can hardly be said to be alive; but if it is dead it has been very neatly embalmed. The hand of the restorer rests on it constantly; but this artist has not, as at Carcassonne, had miracles to accomplish. The interior is very still and empty, with small stony, whitewashed streets, tenanted by a stray dog, a stray cat, a stray old woman. In the middle is a little *place*, with two or three cafes decorated by wide awnings, a little *place* of which the principal feature is a very bad bronze statue of Saint Louis by Pradier. It is almost as bad as the breakfast I had at the inn that bears the name of that pious monarch. You may walk round the *enceinte* of Aigues-Mortes, both outside and in; but you may not, as at Carcassonne, make a portion of this circuit on the *chemin de ronde*, the little projecting footway attached to the inner face of the battlements. This footway, wide enough only for a single pedestrian, is in the best order, and near each of the gates a flight of steps leads up to it; but a locked gate, at the top of the steps, makes access impossible, or at least unlawful. Aigues-Mortes, however, has its citadel, an immense tower, larger than any of the others, a little detached, and standing at the north-west angle of the town.

I called upon the *casernier*, the custodian of the walls, and in his absence I was conducted through this big Tour de Constance by his wife, a very mild, meek woman, yellow with the traces of fever and ague – a scourge which, as might be expected in a town whose name denotes 'dead waters', enters freely at the nine gates. The Tour de Constance is of extraordinary girth and solidity, divided into three superposed circular chambers, with very fine vaults, which are lighted by embrasures of prodigious depth, converging to windows little larger than loopholes. The place served for years as a prison to many of the Protestants of the south whom the revocation of the Edict of Nantes had exposed to atrocious penalties, and the annals of these dreadful chambers during the first half of the last century were written in tears and blood. Some of the recorded cases of long confinement there make one marvel afresh at what man has inflicted and endured. In a country in which a policy of extermination was to be put into practice this horrible tower was an obvious resource. From the battlements at the top, which is surmounted by an old disused lighthouse, you see the little compact rectangular town, which looks hardly bigger than a garden-patch, mapped out beneath you, and follow the plain configuration of its defences. You take possession of it, and you feel that you will remember it always.

V

After this I was free to look about me at Nîmes, and I did so with such attention as the place appeared to require. At the risk of seeming too easily and too frequently disappointed, I will say that it required rather less than I had been prepared to give. It is a town of three or four fine features, rather than a town with, as I may say, a general figure. In general, Nîmes is poor; its only treasures are its Roman remains, which are of the first order. The new French fashions prevail in many of its streets; the old houses are paltry, and the good houses are new; while beside my hotel rose a big spick-and-span church, which had the oddest air of having been intended for Brooklyn or Cleveland. It is true that this church looked out on a square completely French, a square of a fine modern disposition, flanked on one side by a classical *palais de justice* embellished with trees and parapets, and occupied in the centre with a group of allegorical statues, such as one encounters only in the cities of France, the chief of these being a colossal figure by Pradier, representing Nîmes. An English, an American, town which should have such a monument, such a square, as this, would be a place of great pretensions; but like so many little *villes de province* in the country of which I write, Nîmes is easily ornamental. What nobler ornament can there be than the Roman baths at the foot of Mont Cavalier, and the delightful old garden that surrounds them? All that quarter of Nîmes has every reason to be proud of itself; it has been revealed to the world at large by copious photography. A clear, abundant stream gushes from the foot of a high hill (covered with trees and laid out in paths), and is distributed into basins which sufficiently refer themselves to the period that gave them birth – the period that has left its stamp on that pompous Peyrou which we admired at Montpellier. Here are the same terraces and steps and balustrades, and a system of waterworks less impressive, perhaps, but very ingenious and charming. The whole place is a mixture of old Rome and of the

French eighteenth century; for the remains of the antique baths are in a measure incorporated in the modern fountains. In a corner of this umbrageous precinct stands a small Roman ruin, which is known as a temple of Diana, but was more apparently a *nymphaeum*, and appears to have had a graceful connection with the adjacent baths. I learn from Murray that this little temple, of the period of Augustus, 'was reduced to its present state of ruin in 1577'; the moment at which the townspeople, threatened with a siege by the troops of the crown, partly demolished it, lest it should serve as a cover to the enemy. The remains are very fragmentary, but they serve to show that the place was lovely. I spent half an hour in it on a perfect Sunday morning (it is enclosed by a high *grille*, carefully tended, and has a warden of its own), and with the help of my imagination tried to reconstruct a little the aspect of things in the Gallo-Roman days. I do wrong, perhaps, to say that I *tried*; from a flight so deliberate I should have shrunk. But there was a certain contagion of antiquity in the air; and among the ruins of baths and temples, in the very spot where the aqueduct that crosses the Gardon in the wondrous manner I had seen discharged itself, the picture of a splendid paganism seemed vaguely to glow. Roman baths, Roman baths; those words alone were a scene. Everything was changed: I was strolling in a *jardin français*; the bosky slope of the Mont Cavalier (a very modest mountain), hanging over the place, is crowned with a shapeless tower, which is as likely to be of mediaeval as of antique origin; and yet, as I leaned on the parapet of one of the fountains, where a flight of curved steps (a hemicycle, as the French say) descended into a basin full of dark, cool recesses, where the slabs of the Roman foundations gleam through the clear green water, as in this attitude I surrendered myself to contemplation and reverie, it seemed to me that I touched for a moment the ancient world. Such moments are illuminating, and the light of this one mingles, in my memory, with the dusky greenness of the Jardin de la Fontaine.

The fountain proper – the source of all these distributed waters – is the prettiest thing in the world, a reduced copy of Vaucluse. It gushes up at the foot of the Mont Cavalier, at a point where that eminence rises with a certain cliff-like effect, and, like other springs in the same circumstances, appears to issue from the rock with a sort of quivering stillness. I trudged up the Mont Cavalier – it is a matter of five minutes – and having committed this cockneyism enhanced it presently by another. I ascended the stupid Tour Magne, the mysterious structure I mentioned a moment ago. The only feature of this dateless tube, except the inevitable collection of photographs to which you are introduced by the door-keeper, is the view you enjoy from its summit. This view is, of course, remarkably fine, but I am ashamed to say I have not the smallest recollection of it; for while I looked into the brilliant spaces of the air I seemed still to see only what I saw in the depths of the Roman baths – the image, disastrously confused and vague, of a vanished world. This world, however, has left at Nîmes a far more considerable memento than a few old stones covered with water-moss. The Roman arena is the rival of those of Verona and of Arles; at a respectful distance it emulates the Colosseum. It is a small Colosseum, if I may be allowed the expression, and is in a much better preservation than the great circus at Rome. This is especially true of the external walls, with their arches, pillars, cornices. I must add that one should not speak of preservation, in regard to the arena at Nîmes, without speaking also of repair. After the great ruin ceased to be despoiled, it began to be protected, and most of its wounds have been dressed with new material. These matters concern the archaeologist; and I felt here, as I felt afterwards at Arles, that one of the profane, in the presence of such a monument, can only admire and hold his tongue. The great impression, on the whole, is an impression of wonder that so much should have survived. What remains at Nîmes, after all dilapidation is estimated, is astounding. I spent an hour in the *Arènes* on that same sweet Sunday morning, as

I came back from the Roman baths, and saw that the corridors, the vaults, the staircases, the external casing, are still virtually there. Many of these parts are wanting in the Colosseum, whose sublimity of size, however, can afford to dispense with detail. The seats at Nîmes, like those at Verona, have been largely renewed; not that this mattered much, as I lounged on the cool surface of one of them, and admired the mighty concavity of the place and the elliptical skyline, broken by uneven blocks and forming the rim of the monstrous cup – a cup that had been filled with horrors. And yet I made my reflections; I said to myself that though a Roman arena is one of the most impressive of the works of man, it has a touch of that same stupidity which I ventured to discover in the Pont du Gard. It is brutal; it is monotonous; it is not at all exquisite. The *Arènes* at Nîmes were arranged for a bullfight – a form of recreation that, as I was informed, is much *dans les habitudes Nimoises*, and very common throughout Provence, where (still according to my information) it is the usual pastime of a Sunday afternoon. At Arles and Nîmes it has a characteristic setting, but in the villages the patrons of the game make a circle of carts and barrels, on which the spectators perch themselves. I was surprised at the prevalence, in mild Provence, of the Iberian vice, and hardly know whether it makes the custom more respectable that at Nîmes and Arles the thing is shabbily and imperfectly done. The bulls are rarely killed, and indeed often are bulls only in the Irish sense of the term, being domestic and motherly cows. Such an entertainment of course does not supply to the arena that element of the exquisite which I spoke of as wanting. The exquisite at Nîmes is mainly represented by the famous Maison Carrée. The first impression you receive from this delicate little building, as you stand before it, is that you have already seen it many times. Photographs, engravings, models, medals, have placed it definitely in your eye, so that from the sentiment with which you regard it curiosity and surprise are almost completely, and perhaps deplorably, absent. Admiration remains, however, admiration of a familiar and even slightly patronizing kind. The Maison Carrée does not overwhelm you; you can conceive it. It is not one of the great sensations of the antique art; but it is perfectly felicitous, and, in spite of having been put to all sorts of incongruous uses, marvellously preserved. Its slender columns, its delicate proportions, its charming compactness, seemed to bring one nearer to the century that built it than the great superpositions of arenas and bridges, and give it the interest that vibrates from one age to another when the note of taste is struck. If anything were needed to make this little toy-temple a happy production, the service would be rendered by the second-rate boulevard that conducts to it, adorned with inferior cafes and tobacco-shops. Here, in a respectable recess, surrounded by vulgar habitations, and with the theatre, of a classic pretension, opposite, stands the small 'square house', so called because it is much longer than it is broad. I saw it first in the evening, in the vague moonlight, which made it look as if it were cast in bronze. Stendhal says, justly, that it has the shape of a playing card, and he expresses his admiration for it by the singular wish that an 'exact copy' of it should be erected in Paris. He even goes so far as to say that in the year 1880 this tribute will have been rendered to its charms; nothing would be more simple, to his mind, than to 'have' in that city 'le Panthéon de Rome, quelques temples de Grèce'. Stendhal found it amusing to write in the character of a *commis-voyageur*, and sometimes it occurs to his reader that he really was one.

VI

On my way from Nîmes to Arles, I spent three hours at Tarascon; chiefly for the love of Alphonse Daudet, who has written nothing more genial than *Les Aventures Prodigieuses de Tartarin*, and the story of the 'siege' of the bright, dead little town (a mythic siege by the Prussians) in the 'Conies du Lundi'. In the introduction which, for the new edition of his works, he has lately supplied to *Tartarin*, the author of this extravagant but kindly satire gives some account of the displeasure with which he has been visited by the ticklish Tarasconnais. Daudet relates that in his attempt to shed a humorous light upon some of the more erratic phases of the Provençal character, he selected Tarascon at a venture; not because the temperament of its natives is more vainglorious than that of their neighbors, or their rebellion against the 'despotism of fact' more marked, but simply because he had to name a particular Provençal city. Tartarin is a hunter of lions and charmer of women, a true *'produit du midi'*, as Daudet says, who has the most fantastic and fabulous adventures. He is a minimized Don Quixote, with much less dignity, but with equal good faith; and the story of his exploits is a little masterpiece of the light comical. The Tarasconnais, however, declined to take the joke, and opened the vials of their wrath upon the mocking child of Nîmes, who would have been better employed, they doubtless thought, in showing up the infirmities of his own family. I am bound to add that when I passed through Tarascon they did not appear to be in the least out of humor. Nothing could have been brighter, softer, more suggestive of amiable indifference, than the picture it presented to my mind. It lies quietly beside the Rhone, looking across at Beaucaire, which seems very distant and independent, and tacitly consenting to let the castle of the good King René of Anjou, which projects very boldly into the river, pass for its most interesting feature. The other features are, primarily, a sort of vivid sleepiness in the aspect of the place, as if the September noon (it had lingered on into October) lasted longer there than elsewhere; certain low arcades, which make the streets look gray and exhibit empty vistas; and a very curious and beautiful walk beside the Rhone, denominated the Chaussée, a long and narrow causeway, densely shaded by two rows of magnificent old trees, planted in its embankment, and rendered doubly effective, at the moment I passed over it, by a little train of collegians, who had been taken out for mild exercise by a pair of young priests. Lastly, one may say that a striking element of Tarascon, as of any town that lies on the Rhone, is simply the Rhone itself: the big brown flood, of uncertain temper, which has never taken time to forget that it is a child of the mountain and the glacier, and that such an origin carries with it great privileges. Later, at Avignon, I observed it in the exercise of these privileges, chief among which was that of frightening the good people of the old papal city half out of their wits.

The chateau of King René serves today as the prison of a district, and the traveller who wishes to look into it must obtain his permission at the *Mairie of Tarascon*. If he have had a certain experience of French manners, his application will be accompanied with the forms of a considerable obsequiosity, and in this case his request will be granted as civilly as it has been made. The castle has more of the air of a severely feudal fortress than I should suppose the period of its construction (the first half of the fifteenth century) would have warranted; being tremendously bare and perpendicular, and constructed for comfort only in the sense that it was arranged for defence. It is a square and simple mass, composed of small yellow stones, and perched on a pedestal of rock which easily commands the river. The building has the usual circular towers at the corners, and a heavy cornice at the top, and immense stretches of sun-scorched wall, relieved at wide intervals by small windows, heavily cross-barred. It has, above all, an extreme steepness of aspect; I cannot express it otherwise. The walls are as sheer and inhospitable as precipices. The castle has kept its large moat, which is now a hollow filled with wild plants. To this tall fortress the good René retired in the middle of the fifteenth century, finding it apparently the most substantial thing left him in a dominion which had included Naples and Sicily, Lorraine and Anjou. He had been a much-tried monarch and the sport of a various fortune, fighting half his life for thrones he didn't care for, and exalted only to be quickly cast down. Provence was the country of his affection, and the memory of his troubles did not prevent him from holding a joyous court at Tarascon and at Aix. He finished the castle at Tarascon, which had been begun earlier in the century, finished it, I suppose, for consistency's sake, in the manner in which it had originally been designed rather than in accordance with the artistic tastes that formed the consolation of his old age. He was a painter, a writer, a dramatist, a modern dilettante, addicted to private theatricals. There is something very attractive in the image that he has imprinted on the page of history. He was both clever and kind, and many reverses and much suffering had not imbittered him nor quenched his faculty of enjoyment. He was fond of his sweet Provence, and his sweet Provence has been grateful; it has woven a light tissue of legend around the memory of the good King René.

I strolled over his dusky habitation – it must have taken all his good humor to light it up – at the heels of the custodian, who showed me the usual number of castle properties: a deep, well-like court; a collection of winding staircases and vaulted chambers, the embrasures of whose windows and the recesses of whose doorways reveal a tremendous thickness of wall. These things constitute the general identity of old castles; and when one has wandered through a good many, with due discretion of step and protrusion of head, one ceases very much to distinguish and remember, and contents oneself with consigning them to the honorable limbo of the romantic. I must add that this reflection did not the least deter me from crossing the bridge which connects Tarascon with Beaucaire, in order to examine the old

fortress whose ruins adorn the latter city. It stands on a founda-
tion of rock much higher than that of Tarascon, and looks over
with a melancholy expression at its better-conditioned brother.
Its position is magnificent, and its outline very gallant. I was
well rewarded for my pilgrimage; for if the castle of Beaucaire
is only a fragment, the whole place, with its position and its
views, is an ineffaceable picture. It was the stronghold of the
Montmorencys, and its last tenant was that rash Duke François,
whom Richelieu, seizing every occasion to trample on a great
noble, caused to be beheaded at Toulouse, where we saw, in
the Capitol, the butcher's knife with which the cardinal pruned
the crown of France of its thorns. The castle, after the death of
this victim, was virtually demolished. Its site, which Nature
today has taken again to herself, has an extraordinary charm.
The mass of rock that it formerly covered rises high above the
town, and is as precipitous as the side of the Rhone. A tall rusty
iron gate admits you from a quiet corner of Beaucaire to a wild
tangled garden, covering the side of the hill – for the whole
place forms the public promenade of the townsfolk – a garden
without flowers, with little steep, rough paths that wind under a
plantation of small, scrubby stone-pines. Above this is the grassy
platform of the castle, enclosed on one side only (toward the
river) by a large fragment of wall and a very massive dungeon.
There are benches placed in the lee of the wall, and others on
the edge of the platform, where one may enjoy a view, beyond
the river, of certain peeled and scorched undulations. A sweet
desolation, an everlasting peace, seemed to hang in the air. A
very old man (a fragment, like the castle itself) emerged from
some crumbling corner to do me the honors, a very gentle,
obsequious, tottering, toothless, grateful old man. He beguiled
me into an ascent of the solitary tower, from which you may
look down on the big sallow river and glance at diminished
Tarascon, and the barefaced, bald-headed hills behind it. It may
appear that I insist too much upon the nudity of the Provençal
horizon, too much, considering that I have spoken of the

prospect from the heights of Beaucaire as lovely. But it is an exquisite bareness; it seems to exist for the purpose of allowing one to follow the delicate lines of the hills, and touch with the eyes, as it were, the smallest inflections of the landscape. It makes the whole thing seem wonderfully bright and pure.

Beaucaire used to be the scene of a famous fair, the great fair of the south of France. It has gone the way of most fairs, even in France, where these delightful exhibitions hold their own much better than might be supposed. It is still held in the month of July; but the bourgeoises of Tarascon send to the Magasins du Louvre for their smart dresses, and the principal glory of the scene is its long tradition. Even now, however, it ought to be the prettiest of all fairs, for it takes place in a charming wood which lies just beneath the castle, beside the Rhone. The booths, the barracks, the platforms of the mountebanks, the bright-colored crowd, diffused through this midsummer shade, and spotted here and there with the rich Provençal sunshine must be of the most pictorial effect. It is highly probable, too, that it offers a large collection of pretty faces; for even in the few hours that I spent at Tarascon I discovered symptoms of the purity of feature for which the women of the *pays d'Arles* are renowned. The Arlesian headdress, was visible in the streets; and this delightful coiffure is so associated with a charming facial oval, a dark mild eye, a straight Greek nose, and a mouth worthy of all the rest, that it conveys a presumption of beauty which gives the wearer time either to escape or to please you. I have read somewhere, however, that Tarascon is supposed to produce handsome men, as Arles is known to deal in handsome women. It may be that I should have found the Tarasconnais very fine fellows, if I had encountered enough specimens to justify an induction. But there were very few males in the streets, and the place presented no appearance of activity. Here and there the black coif of an old woman or of a young girl was framed by a low doorway; but for the rest, as I have said, Tarascon was mostly involved in a siesta. There was not a creature in the little church of Saint Martha, which I made a point of visiting before I returned to the station, and which, with its fine Romanesque sideportal and its pointed and crocketed Gothic spire, is as curious as it need be, in view of its tradition. It stands in a quiet corner where the grass grows between the small cobblestones, and you pass beneath a deep archway to reach it. The tradition relates that Saint Martha tamed with her own hands, and attached to her girdle, a dreadful dragon, who was known as the Tarasque, and is reported to have given his name to the city on whose site (amid the rocks which form the base of the chateau) he had his cavern. The dragon, perhaps, is the symbol of a ravening paganism, dispelled by the eloquence of a sweet evangelist. The bones of the interesting saint, at all events, were found, in the eleventh century, in a cave beneath the spot on which her altar now stands. I know not what had become of the bones of the dragon.

VII

There are two shabby old inns at Arles, which compete closely for your custom. I mean by this that if you elect to go to the Hôtel du Forum, the Hôtel du Nord, which is placed exactly beside it (at a right angle) watches your arrival with ill-concealed disapproval; and if you take the chances of its neighbor, the Hôtel du Forum seems to glare at you invidiously from all its windows and doors. I forget which of these establishments I selected; whichever it was, I wished very much that it had been the other. The two stand together on the Place des Hommes, a little public square of Arles, which somehow quite misses its effect. As a city, indeed, Arles quite misses its effect in every way; and if it is a charming place, as I think it is, I can hardly tell the reason why. The straight-nosed Arlesiennes account for it in some degree; and the remainder may be charged to the ruins of the arena and the theatre. Beyond this, I remember with affection the ill-proportioned little Place des Hommes; not at all monumental, and given over to puddles and to shabby cafes. I recall with tenderness the tortuous and featureless streets, which looked like the streets of a village, and were paved with villanous little sharp stones, making all exercise penitential. Consecrated by association is even a tiresome walk that I took the evening I arrived, with the purpose of obtaining a view of the Rhone. I had been to Arles before, years ago, and it seemed to me that I remembered finding on the banks of the stream some sort of picture. I think that on the evening of which I speak there was a watery moon, which it seemed to me would light up the past as well as the present. But I found no picture, and I scarcely found the Rhone at all. I lost my way, and there was not a creature in the streets to whom I could appeal. Nothing could be more provincial than the situation of Arles at ten o'clock at night. At last I arrived at a kind of embankment, where I could see the great mud-colored stream slipping along in the soundless darkness. It had come on to rain, I know not what had happened to the moon, and the whole place was anything but gay. It was not what I had looked for; what I had looked for was in the irrecoverable past. I groped my way back to the inn over the infernal *cailloux*, feeling like a discomfited Dogberry. I remember now that this hotel was the one (whichever that may be) which has the fragment of a Gallo-Roman portico inserted into one of its angles. I had chosen it for the sake of this exceptional ornament. It was damp and dark, and the floors felt gritty to the feet; it was an establishment at which the dreadful *gras-double* might have appeared at the table d'hôte, as it had done at Narbonne. Nevertheless, I was glad to get back to it; and nevertheless, too – and this is the moral of my simple anecdote – my pointless little walk (I don't speak of the pavement) suffuses itself, as I look back upon it, with a romantic tone. And in relation to the inn, I suppose I had better mention that I am well aware of the inconsistency of a person who dislikes the modern caravansary, and yet grumbles when he finds a hotel of the superannuated sort. One ought to choose, it would seem, and make the best of either alternative. The two old taverns at Arles are quite unimproved; such as they must have been in the infancy of the modern world, when Stendhal passed that way, and the lumbering diligence deposited him in the Place des Hommes, such in every detail they are today. *Vieilles auberges de France*, one ought to enjoy their gritty floors and greasy windowpanes. Let it be put on record, therefore, that I have been, I won't say less comfortable, but at least less happy, at better inns.

To be really historic, I should have mentioned that before going to look for the Rhone I had spent part of the evening on the opposite side of the little *place*, and that I indulged in this recreation for two definite reasons. One of these was that I had an opportunity of conversing at a cafe with an attractive young Englishman, whom I had met in the afternoon at Tarascon, and more remotely, in other years, in London; the other was that there sat enthroned behind the counter a splendid mature

Arlesienne, whom my companion and I agreed that it was a rare privilege to contemplate. There is no rule of good manners or morals which makes it improper, at a cafe, to fix one's eyes upon the *dame de comptoir*; the lady is, in the nature of things, a part of your *consommation*. We were therefore free to admire without restriction the handsomest person I had ever seen give change for a five-franc piece. She was a large quiet woman, who would never see forty again; of an intensely feminine type, yet wonderfully rich and robust, and full of a certain physical nobleness. Though she was not really old, she was antique, and she was very grave, even a little sad. She had the dignity of a Roman empress, and she handled coppers as if they had been stamped with the head of Caesar. I have seen washerwomen in the Trastevere who were perhaps as handsome as she; but even the headdress of the Roman contadina contributes less to the dignity of the person born to wear it than the sweet and stately Arlesian cap, which sits at once aloft and on the back of the head; which is accompanied with a wide black bow covering a considerable part of the crown; and which, finally, accommodates itself indescribably well to the manner in which the tresses of the front are pushed behind the ears.

This admirable dispenser of lumps of sugar has distracted me a little; for I am still not sufficiently historical. Before going to the cafe I had dined, and before dining I had found time to go and look at the arena. Then it was that I discovered that Arles has no general physiognomy, and, except the delightful little church of Saint Trophimus, no architecture, and that the rugosities of its dirty lanes affect the feet like knife-blades. It was not then, on the other hand, that I saw the arena best. The second day of my stay at Arles I devoted to a pilgrimage to the strange old hill town of Les Baux, the mediaeval Pompeii, of which I shall give myself the pleasure of speaking. The evening of that day, however (my friend and I returned in time for a late dinner), I wandered among the Roman remains of the place by the light of a magnificent moon, and gathered an impression which has lost little of its silvery glow. The moon of the evening before had been aqueous and erratic; but if on the present occasion it was guilty of any irregularity, the worst it did was only to linger beyond its time in the heavens, in order to let us look at things comfortably. The effect was admirable; it brought back the impression of the way, in Rome itself, on evenings like that, the moonshine rests upon broken shafts and slabs of antique pavement. As we sat in the theatre, looking at the two lone columns that survive – part of the decoration of the back of the stage – and at the fragments of ruin around them, we might have been in the Roman forum. The arena at Arles, with its great magnitude, is less complete than that of Nîmes; it has suffered even more the assaults of time and of the children of time, and it has been less repaired. The seats are almost wholly wanting; but the external walls minus the topmost tier of arches, are massively, ruggedly, complete; and the vaulted corridors seem as solid as the day they were built. The whole thing is superbly vast, and as monumental, for place of light amusement – what is called in America a 'variety show' – as it entered only into the Roman mind to make such establishments. The *podium* is much higher than at Nîmes, and many of the great white slabs that faced it have been recovered and put into their places. The proconsular box has been more or less reconstructed, and the great converging passages of approach to it are still majestically distinct: so that, as I sat there in the moon-charmed stillness, leaning my elbows on the battered parapet of the ring, it was not impossible to listen to the murmurs and shudders, the thick voice of the circus, that died away fifteen hundred years ago.

The theatre has a voice as well, but it lingers on the ear of time with a different music. The Roman theatre at Arles seemed to me one of the most charming and touching ruins I had ever beheld; I took a particular fancy to it. It is less than a skeleton – the arena may be called a skeleton; for it consists only of half a dozen bones. The traces of the row of columns which formed the scene – the permanent back-scene – remain; two marble pillars – I just

mentioned them – are upright, with a fragment of their entabla-
ture. Before them is the vacant space which was filled by the stage,
with the line of the proscenium distinct, marked by a deep groove,
impressed upon slabs of stone, which looks as if the bottom of a
high screen had been intended to fit into it. The semicircle formed
by the seats – half a cup – rises opposite; some of the rows are
distinctly marked. The floor, from the bottom of the stage, in the
shape of an arc of which the chord is formed by the line of the
orchestra, is covered by slabs of colored marble – red, yellow,
and green – which, though terribly battered and cracked today,
give one an idea of the elegance of the interior. Everything shows
that it was on a great scale: the large sweep of its enclosing walls,
the massive corridors that passed behind the auditorium, and of
which we can still perfectly take the measure. The way in which
every seat commanded the stage is a lesson to the architects of our
epoch, as also the immense size of the place is a proof of extraordinary power of voice on the part of the Roman actors. It was after
we had spent half an hour in the moonshine at the arena that we
came on to this more ghostly and more exquisite ruin. The principal entrance was locked, but we effected an easy *escalade*, scaled
a low parapet, and descended into the place behind the scenes. It
was as light as day, and the solitude was complete. The two slim
columns, as we sat on the broken benches, stood there like a pair
of silent actors. What I called touching, just now, was the thought
that here the human voice, the utterance of a great language, had
been supreme. The air was full of intonations and cadences; not
of the echo of smashing blows, of riven armor, of howling victims
and roaring beasts. The spot is, in short, one of the sweetest lega-
cies of the ancient world; and there seems no profanation in the
fact that by day it is open to the good people of Arles, who use it
to pass, by no means in great numbers, from one part of the town
to the other; treading the old marble floor, and brushing, if need
be, the empty benches. This familiarity does not kill the place
again; it makes it, on the contrary, live a little, makes the present
and the past touch each other.

VIII

The third lion of Arles has nothing to do with the ancient world, but only with the old one. The church of Saint Trophimus, whose wonderful Romanesque porch is the principal ornament of the principal *place*, – a *place* otherwise distinguished by the presence of a slim and tapering obelisk in the middle, as well as by that of the hôtel de ville and the museum – the interesting church of Saint Trophimus swears a little, as the French say, with the peculiar character of Arles. It is very remarkable, but I would rather it were in another place. Arles is delightfully pagan, and Saint Trophimus, with its apostolic sculptures, is rather a false note. These sculptures are equally remarkable for their primitive vigor and for the perfect preservation in which they have come down to us. The deep recess of a round-arched porch of the twelfth century is covered with quaint figures, which have not lost a nose or a finger. An angular, Byzantine-looking Christ sits in a diamond-shaped frame at the summit of the arch, surrounded by little angels, by great apostles, by winged beasts, by a hundred sacred symbols and grotesque ornaments. It is a dense embroidery of sculpture, black with time, but as uninjured as if it had been kept under glass. One good mark for the French Revolution! Of the interior of the church, which has a nave of the twelfth century, and a choir three hundred years more recent, I chiefly remember the odd feature that the Romanesque aisles are so narrow that you literally – or almost – squeeze through them. You do so with some eagerness, for your natural purpose is to pass out to the cloister. This cloister, as distinguished and as perfect as the porch, has a great deal of charm. Its four sides, which are not of the same period (the earliest and best are of the twelfth century), have an elaborate arcade, supported on delicate pairs of columns, the capitals of which show an extraordinary variety of device and ornament. At the corners of the quadrangle these columns take the form of curious human figures. The whole thing is a gem of lightness and preservation, and is often cited for its beauty; but – if it doesn't sound too profane – I prefer, especially at Arles, the ruins of the Roman theatre. The antique element is too precious to be mingled with anything less rare. This truth was very present to my mind during a ramble of a couple of hours that I took just before leaving the place; and the glowing beauty of the morning gave the last touch of the impression. I spent half an hour at the Museum; then I took another look at the Roman theatre; after which I walked a little out of the town to the Alyscamps, the old Elysian Fields, the meagre remnant of the old pagan place of sepulture, which was afterwards used by the Christians, but has been for ages deserted, and now consists only of a melancholy avenue of cypresses, lined with a succession of ancient sarcophagi, empty, mossy, and mutilated. An iron-foundry, or some horrible establishment which is conditioned upon tall chimneys and a noise of hammering and banging, has been established near at hand; but the cypresses shut it out well enough, and this small patch of Elysium is a very romantic corner.

The door of the museum stands ajar, and a vigilant custodian, with the usual batch of photographs on his mind, peeps out at you disapprovingly while you linger opposite, before the charming portal of Saint Trophimus, which you may look at for nothing. When you succumb to the silent influence of his eye, and go over to visit his collection, you find yourself in a desecrated church, in which a variety of ancient objects, disinterred in Arlesian soil, have been arranged without any pomp. The best of these, I believe, were found in the ruins of the theatre. Some of the most curious of them are early Christian sarcophagi, exactly on the pagan model, but covered with rude yet vigorously wrought images of the apostles, and with illustrations of scriptural history. Beauty of the highest kind, either of conception or of execution, is absent from most of the Roman fragments, which belong to the taste of a late period and a provincial civilization. But a gulf divides them from the bristling little imagery of the Christian sarcophagi, in which, at the same time, one detects a vague emulation of the rich examples by which their authors were surrounded. There is a certain element of style in all the pagan things; there is not a hint of it in the early Christian relics, among which, according to M. Joanne, of the *Guide*, are to be found more fine sarcophagi than in any collection but that of St John Lateran. In two or three of the Roman fragments there is a noticeable distinction; principally in a charming bust of a boy, quite perfect, with those salient eyes that one sees in certain antique busts, and to which the absence of vision in the marble mask gives a look, often very touching, as of a baffled effort to see; also in the head of a woman, found in the ruins of the theatre, who, alas! has lost her nose, and whose noble, simple contour, barring this deficiency, recalls the great manner of the Venus of Milo. There are various rich architectural fragments which indicate that that edifice was a very splendid affair. This little Museum at Arles, in short, is the most Roman thing I know of, out of Rome.

IX

I find that I declared one evening, in a little journal I was keeping at that time, that I was weary of writing (I was probably very sleepy), but that it was essential I should make some note of my visit to Les Baux. I must have gone to sleep as soon as I had recorded this necessity, for I search my small diary in vain for any account of that enchanting spot. I have nothing but my memory to consult – a memory which is fairly good in regard to a general impression, but is terribly infirm in the matter of details and items. We knew in advance, my companion and I, that Les Baux was a pearl of picturesqueness; for had we not read as much in the handbook of Murray, who has the testimony of an English nobleman as to its attractions? We also knew that it lay some miles from Arles, on the crest of the Alpilles, the craggy little mountains which, as I stood on the breezy platform of Beaucaire, formed to my eye a charming, if somewhat remote, background to Tarascon; this assurance having been given us by the landlady of the inn at Arles, of whom we hired a rather lumbering conveyance. The weather was not promising, but it proved a good day for the mediaeval Pompeii; a gray, melancholy, moist, but rainless, or almost rainless day, with nothing in the sky to flout, as the poet says, the dejected and pulverized past. The drive itself was charming; for there is an inexhaustible sweetness in the gray-green landscape of Provence. It is never absolutely flat, and yet is never really ambitious, and is full both of entertainment and repose.

It is in constant undulation, and the bareness of the soil lends itself easily to outline and profile. When I say the bareness, I mean the absence of woods and hedges. It blooms with heath and scented shrubs and stunted olive; and the white rock shining through the scattered herbage has a brightness which answers to the brightness of the sky. Of course it needs the sunshine, for all southern countries look a little false under the ground glass of incipient bad weather. This was the case on the day of my pilgrimage to Les Baux. Nevertheless, I was as glad to keep going as I was to arrive; and as I went it seemed to me that true happiness would consist in wandering through such a land on foot, on September afternoons, when one might stretch oneself on the warm ground in some shady hollow, and listen to the hum of bees and the whistle of melancholy shepherds; for in Provence the shepherds whistle to their flocks. I saw two or three of them, in the course of this drive to Les Baux, meandering about, looking behind, and calling upon the sheep in this way to follow, which the sheep always did, very promptly, with ovine unanimity. Nothing is more picturesque than to see a slow shepherd threading his way down one of the winding paths on a hillside, with his flock close behind him, necessarily expanded, yet keeping just at his heels, bending and twisting as it goes, and looking rather like the tail of a dingy comet.

About four miles from Arles, as you drive northward toward the Alpilles, of which Alphonse Daudet has spoken so often, and, as he might say, so intimately, stand on a hill that overlooks the road the very considerable ruins of the abbey of Montmajour, one of the innumerable remnants of a feudal and ecclesiastical (as well as an architectural) past that one encounters in the South of France; remnants which, it must be confessed, tend to introduce a certain confusion and satiety into the passive mind of the tourist. Montmajour, however, is very impressive and interesting; the only trouble with it is that, unless you have stopped and returned to Arles, you see it in memory over the head of Les Baux, which is a much more absorbing picture. A part of the mass of buildings (the monastery) dates only from the last century; and the stiff architecture of that period does not lend itself very gracefully to desolation: it looks too much as if it had been burnt down the year before. The monastery was demolished during the Revolution, and it injures a little the effect of the very much more ancient fragments that are connected with it. The whole place is on a great scale; it was a rich and splendid abbey. The church, a vast basilica of the eleventh century, and of the noblest proportions, is virtually intact; I mean as regards its essentials, for the details have completely vanished. The huge solid shell is full of expression; it looks as if it had been hollowed out by the sincerity of early faith, and it opens into a cloister as impressive as itself. Wherever one goes, in France, one meets, looking backward a little, the spectre of the great Revolution; and one meets it always in the shape of the destruction of something beautiful and precious. To make us forgive it at all, how much it must also have destroyed that was more hateful than itself! Beneath the church of Montmajour is a most extraordinary crypt, almost as big as the edifice above it, and making a complete subterranean temple, surrounded with a circular gallery, or deambulatory, which expands at intervals into five square chapels. There are other things, of which I have but a confused memory: a great fortified keep; a queer little primitive chapel, hollowed out of the rock, beneath these later structures, and recommended to the visitor's attention as the confessional of Saint Trophimus, who shares with so many worthies the glory of being the first apostle of the Gauls. Then there is a strange, small church, of the dimmest antiquity, standing at a distance from the other buildings. I remember that after we had let ourselves down a good many steepish places to visit crypts and confessionals, we walked across a field to this archaic cruciform edifice, and went thence to a point further down the road, where our carriage was awaiting us. The chapel of the Holy Cross, as it is called, is classed among the historic monuments of France; and I read in a queer, rambling, ill-written book which I picked up at Avignon, and in which the author, M. Louis de Lainbel, has buried a great deal of curious information on the subject of Provence, under a style inspiring little confidence, that the 'délicieuse chapelle de Sainte-Croix' is a 'véritable bijou artistique'. He speaks of 'a piece of lace in stone', which runs from one end of the building to the other, but of which I am obliged to confess that I have no recollection. I retain, however, a sufficiently clear impression of the little superannuated temple, with its four apses and its perceptible odor of antiquity – the odor of the eleventh century.

The ruins of Les Baux remain quite indistinguishable, even when you are directly beneath them, at the foot of the charming little Alpilles, which mass themselves with a kind of delicate ruggedness. Rock and ruin have been so welded together by the confusions of time, that as you approach it from behind – that is, from the direction of Arles – the place presents simply a general air of cragginess. Nothing can be prettier than the crags of Provence; they are beautifully modelled, as painters say, and they have a delightful silvery color. The road winds round the foot of the hills on the top of which Les Baux is planted, and passes into another valley, from which the approach to the town is many degrees less precipitous, and may be comfortably made in a carriage. Of course the deeply inquiring traveller will alight as promptly as possible; for the pleasure of climbing into this queerest of cities on foot is not the least part of the entertainment of going there. Then you appreciate its extraordinary position, its picturesqueness, its steepness, its desolation and decay. It hangs – that is, what remains of it – to the slanting summit of the mountain. Nothing would be more natural than for the whole place to roll down into the valley. A part of it has done so – for it is not unjust to suppose that in the process of decay the crumbled particles have sought the lower level; while the remainder still clings to its magnificent perch.

If I called Les Baux a city, just above, it was not that I was stretching a point in favor of the small spot which today contains but a few dozen inhabitants. The history of the place is as extraordinary as its situation. It was not only a city, but a state; not only a state, but an empire; and on the crest of its little mountain called itself sovereign of a territory, or at least of scattered towns and counties, with which its present aspect is grotesquely out of relation. The lords of Les Baux, in a word, were great feudal proprietors; and there was a time during which the island of Sardinia, to say nothing of places nearer home, such as Arles and Marseilles, paid them homage. The chronicle of this old Provençal house has been written, in a style somewhat unctuous and flowery, by M. Jules Canonge. I purchased the little book – a modest pamphlet – at the establishment of the good sisters, just beside the church, in one of the highest parts of Les Baux. The sisters have a school for the hardy little Baussenques, whom I heard piping their lessons, while I waited in the cold *parloir* for one of the ladies to come and speak to me. Nothing could have been more perfect than the manner of this excellent woman when she arrived; yet her small religious house seemed a very out-of-the-way corner of the world. It was spotlessly neat, and the rooms looked as if they had lately been papered and painted: in this respect, at the mediaeval Pompeii, they were rather a discord. They were, at any rate, the newest, freshest thing at Les Baux. I remember going round to the church, after I had left the good sisters, and to a little quiet terrace, which stands in front of it, ornamented with a few small trees and bordered with a wall, breast-high, over which you look down steep hillsides, off into the air and all about the neighboring country. I remember saying to myself that this little terrace was one of those felicitous nooks which the tourist of taste keeps in his mind as a picture. The church was small and brown and dark, with a certain rustic richness. All this, however, is no general description of Les Baux.

I am unable to give any coherent account of the place, for the simple reason that it is a mere confusion of ruin. It has not been preserved in lava like Pompeii, and its streets and houses, its ramparts and castle, have become fragmentary, not through the sudden destruction, but through the gradual withdrawal, of a population. It is not an extinguished, but a deserted city; more deserted far than even Carcassonne and Aigues-Mortes, where I found so much entertainment in the grass-grown element. It is of very small extent, and even in the days of its greatness, when its lords entitled themselves counts of Cephalonia and

Neophantis, kings of Arles and Vienne, princes of Achaia, and emperors of Constantinople – even at this flourishing period, when, as M. Jules Canonge remarks, 'they were able to depress the balance in which the fate of peoples and kings is weighed,' the plucky little city contained at the most no more than thirty-six hundred souls. Yet its lords (who, however, as I have said, were able to present a long list of subject towns, most of them, though a few are renowned, unknown to fame) were seneschals and captains-general of Piedmont and Lombardy, grand admirals of the kingdom of Naples, and its ladies were sought in marriage by half the first princes in Europe. A considerable part of the little narrative of M. Canonge is taken up with the great alliances of the House of Baux, whose fortunes, matrimonial and other, he traces from the eleventh century down to the sixteenth. The empty shells of a considerable number of old houses, many of which must have been superb, the lines of certain steep little streets, the foundations of a castle, and ever so many splendid views, are all that remains today of these great titles. To such a list I may add a dozen very polite and sympathetic people, who emerged from the interstices of the desultory little town to gaze at the two foreigners who had driven over from Arles, and whose horses were being baited at the modest inn. The resources of this establishment we did not venture otherwise to test, in spite of the seductive fact that the sign over the door was in the Provençal tongue. This little group included the baker, a rather melancholy young man, in high boots and a cloak, with whom and his companions we had a good deal of conversation. The Baussenques of today struck me as a very mild and agreeable race, with a good deal of the natural amenity which, on occasions like this one, the traveller, who is, waiting for his horses to be put in or his dinner to be prepared, observes in the charming people who lend themselves to conversation in the hill-towns of Tuscany. The spot where our entertainers at Les Baux congregated was naturally the most inhabited portion of the town; as I say, there were at least a dozen human figures within sight.

Presently we wandered away from them, scaled the higher places, seated ourselves among the ruins of the castle, and looked down from the cliff overhanging that portion of the road which I have mentioned as approaching Les Baux from behind. I was unable to trace the configuration of the castle as plainly as the writers who have described it in the guidebooks, and I am ashamed to say that I did not even perceive the three great figures of stone (the three Marys, as they are called; the two Marys of Scripture, with Martha), which constitute one of the curiosities of the place, and of which M. Jules Canonge speaks with almost hyperbolical admiration. A brisk shower, lasting some ten minutes, led us to take refuge in a cavity, of mysterious origin, where the melancholy baker presently discovered us, having had the *bonne pensée* of coming up for us with an umbrella which certainly belonged, in former ages, to one of the Stéphanettes or Berangères commemorated by M. Canonge. His oven, I am afraid, was cold so long as our visit lasted. When the rain was over we wandered down to the little disencumbered space before the inn, through a small labyrinth of obliterated things. They took the form of narrow, precipitous streets, bordered by empty houses, with gaping windows and absent doors, through which we had glimpses of sculptured chimney pieces and fragments of stately arch and vault. Some of the houses are still inhabited; but most of them are open to the air and weather. Some of them have completely collapsed; others present to the street a front which enables one to judge of the physiognomy of Les Baux in the days of its importance. This importance had pretty well passed away in the early part of the sixteenth century, when the place ceased to be an independent principality. It became – by bequest of one of its lords, Bernardin des Baux, a great captain of his time – part of the appanage of the kings of France, by whom it was placed under the protection of Arles, which had formerly occupied with regard to it a different position. I know not whether the Arlesians neglected their trust; but the extinction of the sturdy little stronghold is too complete not to have begun long ago. Its memories are buried under its ponderous stones. As we drove away from it in the gloaming, my friend and I agreed that the two or three hours we had spent there were among the happiest impressions of a pair of tourists very curious in the picturesque. We almost forgot that we were bound to regret that the shortened day left us no time to drive five miles further, above a pass in the little mountains – it had beckoned to us in the morning, when we came in sight of it, almost irresistibly – to see the Roman arch and mausoleum of Saint Rémy. To compass this larger excursion (including the visit to Les Baux) you must start from Arles very early in the morning; but I can imagine no more delightful day.

X

I had been twice at Avignon before, and yet I was not satisfied. I probably am satisfied now; nevertheless, I enjoyed my third visit. I shall not soon forget the first, on which a particular emotion set indelible stamp. I was travelling northward, in 1870, after four months spent, for the first time, in Italy. It was the middle of January, and I had found myself, unexpectedly, forced to return to England for the rest of the winter. It was an insufferable disappointment; I was wretched and broken-hearted. Italy appeared to me at that time so much better than anything else in the world, that to rise from table in the middle of the feast was a prospect of being hungry for the rest of my days. I had heard a great deal of praise of the south of France; but the south of France was a poor consolation. In this state of mind I arrived at Avignon, which under a bright, hard winter sun was tingling – fairly spinning – with the *mistral*. I find in my journal of the other day a reference to the acuteness of my reluctance in January, 1870. France, after Italy, appeared, in the language of the latter country, *poco simpatica*; and I thought it necessary, for reasons now inconceivable, to read the *Figaro*, which was filled with descriptions of the horrible Troppmann, the murderer of the *famille* Kink. Troppmann, Kink, *le crime de Pantin*, very names that figured in this episode seemed to wave me back. Had I abandoned the sonorous south to associate with vocables so base?

It was very cold, the other day, at Avignon; for though there was no *mistral*, it was raining as it rains in Provence, and the dampness had a terrible chill in it. As I sat by my fire, late at night – for in genial Avignon, in October, I had to have a fire – it came back to me that eleven years before I had at that same hour sat by a fire in that same room, and, writing to a friend to whom I was not afraid to appear extravagant, had made a vow that at some happier period of the future I would avenge myself on the *ci-devant* city of the Popes by taking it in a contrary sense. I suppose that I redeemed my vow on the occasion of my second visit better than on my third; for then I was on my way to Italy, and that vengeance, of course, was complete. The only drawback was that I was in such a hurry to get to Ventimiglia (where the Italian custom house was to be the sign of my triumph), that I scarcely took time to make it clear to myself at Avignon that this was better than reading the *Figaro*. I hurried on almost too fast to enjoy the consciousness of moving southward. On this last occasion I was unfortunately destitute of that happy faith. Avignon was my southernmost limit; after which I was to turn round and proceed back to England. But in the interval I had been a great deal in Italy, and that made all the difference.

I had plenty of time to think of this, for the rain kept me practically housed for the first twenty-four hours. It had been raining in these regions for a month, and people had begun to look askance at the Rhone, though as yet the volume of the river was not exorbitant. The only excursion possible, while the torrent descended, was a kind of horizontal dive, accompanied with infinite splashing, to the little *musée* of the town, which is within a moderate walk of the hotel. I had a memory of it from my first visit; it had appeared to me more pictorial than its pictures. I found that recollection had flattered it a little, and that it is neither better nor worse than most provincial museums. It has the usual musty chill in the air, the usual grass-grown forecourt, in which a few lumpish Roman fragments are disposed, the usual red tiles on the floor, and the usual specimens of the more livid schools on the walls. I rang up the *gardien*, who arrived with a bunch of keys, wiping his mouth; he unlocked doors for me, opened shutters, and while (to my distress, as if the things had been worth lingering over) he shuffled about after me, he announced the names of the pictures before which I stopped, in a voice that reverberated through the melancholy halls, and seemed to make the authorship shameful when it was obscure, and grotesque when it pretended to be great. Then there were intervals of silence, while I stared absent-mindedly, at haphazard, at some indistinguishable canvas, and the only sound was the downpour of the rain on the skylights. The museum of Avignon derives a certain dignity from its Roman fragments. The town has no Roman monuments to show; in this respect, beside its brilliant neighbors, Arles and Nîmes, it is a blank. But a great many small objects have been found in its soil – pottery, glass, bronzes, lamps, vessels and ornaments of gold and silver. The glass is especially charming – small vessels of the most delicate shape and substance, many of them perfectly preserved. These diminutive, intimate things bring one near to the old Roman life; they seem like pearls strung upon the slender thread that swings across the gulf of time. A little glass cup that Roman lips have touched says more to us than the great vessel of an arena. There are two small silver *casseroles*, with chiselled handles, in the museum of Avignon, that struck me as among the most charming survivals of antiquity.

I did wrong just above, to speak of my attack on this establishment as the only recreation I took that first wet day; for I remember a terribly moist visit to the former palace of the Popes, which could have taken place only in the same tempestuous hours. It is true that I scarcely know why I should have gone out to see the papal palace in the rain, for I had been over it twice before, and even then had not found the interest of the place so complete as it ought to be; the fact, nevertheless, remains that this last occasion is much associated with an umbrella, which was not superfluous even in some of the chambers and corridors of the gigantic pile. It had already seemed to me the dreariest of all historical buildings, and my final visit confirmed the impression. The place is as intricate as it is vast, and as desolate as it is dirty. The imagination has, for some reason or other, to make more than the effort usual in such cases to restore and repeople it. The fact, indeed, is simply that the palace has been so incalculably abused and altered. The alterations have been so numerous that, though I have duly conned the enumerations, supplied in guidebooks, of the principal perversions, I do not pretend to carry any of them in my head. The huge bare mass, without ornament, without grace, despoiled of its battlements and defaced with sordid modern windows, covering the Rocher des Doms, and looking down over the Rhone and the broken bridge of Saint-Bénezet (which stops in such a sketchable manner in midstream), and across at the lonely tower of Philippe le Bel and the ruined wall of Villeneuve, makes at a distance, in spite of its poverty, a great figure, the effect of which is carried out by the tower of the church beside it (crowned though the latter be, in a top-heavy fashion, with an immense modern image of the Virgin) and by the thick, dark foliage of the garden laid out on a still higher portion of the eminence. This garden recalls, faintly and a trifle perversely, the grounds of the Pincian at Rome. I know not whether it is the shadow of the papal name, present in both places, combined with a vague analogy between the churches – which, approached in each case by a flight of steps, seemed to defend the precinct – but each time I have seen the Promenade des Doms it has carried my thoughts to the wider and loftier terrace from which you look away at the Tiber and Saint Peter's.

As you stand before the papal palace, and especially as you enter it, you are struck with its being a very dull monument. History enough was enacted here: the great schism lasted from 1305 to 1370, during which seven popes, all Frenchmen, carried on the court of Avignon on principles that have not commended themselves to the esteem of posterity. But history has been whitewashed away, and the scandals of that period have mingled with the dust of dilapidations and repairs. The building has for many years been occupied as a barrack for regiments of the line, and the main characteristics of a barrack – an extreme nudity and a very queer smell – prevail throughout its endless compart-ments. Nothing could have been more cruelly dismal than the appearance it presented at the time of this third visit of mine. A regiment, changing quarters, had departed the day before, and another was expected to arrive (from Algeria) on the morrow. The place had been left in the befouled and belittered condition which marks the passage of the military after they have broken camp, and it would offer but a melancholy welcome to the regiment that was about to take possession. Enormous windows had been left carelessly open all over the building, and the rain and wind were beating into empty rooms and passages; making draughts which purified, perhaps, but which scarcely cheered. For an arrival, it was horrible. A handful of soldiers had remained behind. In one of the big vaulted rooms several of them were lying on their wretched beds, in the dim light, in the cold, in the damp, with the bleak, bare walls before them, and their overcoats, spread over them, pulled up to their noses. I pitied them immensely, though they may have felt less wretched than they looked. I thought not of the old profligacies and crimes, not of the funnel-shaped torture-chamber (which, after exciting the shudder of generations, has been ascertained now, I believe, to have been a mediaeval bakehouse), not of the tower of the *glacière* and the horrors perpetrated here in the Revolution, but of the military burden of young France. One wonders how young France endures it, and one is forced to believe that the French conscript has, in addition to his notorious good humor, greater toughness than is commonly supposed by those who consider only the more relaxing influences of French civilization. I hope he finds occasional compensation for such moments as I saw those damp young peasants passing on the mattresses of their hideous barrack, without anything around to remind them that they were in the most civilized of countries. The only traces of former splendor now visible in the papal pile are the walls and vaults of two small chapels, painted in fresco, so battered and effaced as to be scarcely distinguishable, by Simone Memmi. It offers, of course, a peculiarly good field for restoration, and I believe the government intend to take it in hand. I mention this fact without a sigh; for they cannot well make it less interesting than it is at present.

XI

Fortunately, it did not rain every day (though I believe it was raining everywhere else in the department); otherwise I should not have been able to go to Villeneuve and to Vaucluse. The afternoon, indeed, was lovely when I walked over the interminable bridge that spans the two arms of the Rhone, divided here by a considerable island, and directed my course, like a solitary horseman – on foot, to the lonely tower which forms one of the outworks of Villeneuve-lès-Avignon. The picturesque, half-deserted little town lies a couple of miles further up the river. The immense round towers of its old citadel and the long stretches of ruined wall covering the slope on which it lies, are the most striking features of the nearer view, as you look from Avignon across the Rhone. I spent a couple of hours in visiting these objects, and there was a kind of pictorial sweetness in the episode; but I have not many details to relate. The isolated tower I just mentioned has much in common with the detached donjon of Montmajour, which I had looked at in going to Les Baux, and to which I paid my respects in speaking of that excursion. Also the work of Philippe le Bel (built in 1307), it is amazingly big and stubborn, and formed the opposite limit of the broken bridge, whose first arches (on the side of Avignon) alone remain to give a measure of the occasional volume of the Rhone. Half an hour's walk brought me to Villeneuve, which lies away from the river, looking like a big village, half depopulated, and occupied for the most part by dogs and cats, old women and small children; these last, in general, remarkably pretty, in the manner of the children of Provence. You pass through the place, which seems in a singular degree vague and unconscious, and come to the rounded hill on which the ruined abbey lifts its yellow walls – the Benedictine abbey of Saint-André, at once a church, a monastery, and a fortress. A large part of the crumbling *enceinte* disposes itself over the hill; but for the rest, all that has preserved any traceable cohesion is a considerable portion of the citadel. The defence of the place appears to have been intrusted largely to the huge round towers that flank the old gate; one of which, the more complete, the ancient warden (having first inducted me into his own dusky little apartment, and presented me with a great bunch of lavender) enabled me to examine in detail. I would almost have dispensed with the privilege, for I think I have already mentioned that an acquaintance with many feudal interiors has wrought a sad confusion in my mind. The image of the outside always remains distinct; I keep it apart from other images of the same sort; it makes a picture sufficiently ineffaceable. But the guard-rooms, winding staircases, loopholes, prisons, repeat themselves and intermingle; they have a wearisome family likeness. There are always black passages and corners, and walls twenty feet thick; and there is always some high place to climb up to for the sake of a 'magnificent' view. The views, too, are apt to get muddled. These dense gate-towers of Philippe le Bel struck me, however, as peculiarly wicked and grim. Their capacity is of the largest, and they contain ever so many devilish little dungeons, lighted by the narrowest slit in the prodigious wall, where it comes over one with a good deal of vividness and still more horror that wretched human beings ever lay there rotting in the dark. The dungeons of Villeneuve made a particular impression on me, greater than any, except those of Loches, which must surely be the most gruesome in Europe. I hasten to add that every dark hole at Villeneuve is called a dungeon; and I believe it is well established that in this manner, in almost all old castles and towers, the sensibilities of the modern tourist are unscrupulously played upon. There were plenty of black holes in the Middle Ages that were not dungeons, but household receptacles of various kinds; and many a tear dropped in pity for the groaning captive has really been addressed to the spirits of the larder and the faggot-nook. For all this, there are some very bad corners in the towers of Villeneuve, so that I was not wide of the mark when I began to think again, as

I had often thought before, of the stoutness of the human composition in the Middle Ages, and the tranquillity of nerve of people to whom the groaning captive and the blackness of a 'living tomb' were familiar ideas, which did not at all interfere with their happiness or their sanity. Our modern nerves, our irritable sympathies, our easy discomforts and fears, make one think (in some relations) less respectfully of human nature. Unless, indeed, it be true, as I have heard it maintained, that in the Middle Ages everyone did go mad – everyone *was* mad. The theory that this was a period of general insanity is not altogether indefensible.

Within the old walls of its immense abbey the town of Villeneuve has built itself a rough faubourg; the fragments with which the soil was covered having been, I suppose, a quarry of material. There are no streets; the small, shabby houses, almost hovels, straggle at random over the uneven ground. The only important feature is a convent of cloistered nuns, who have a large garden (always within the walls) behind their house, and whose doleful establishment you look down into, or down at simply, from the battlements of the citadel. One or two of the nuns were passing in and out of the house; they wore gray robes, with a bright red cape. I thought their situation most provincial. I came away, and wandered a little over the base of the hill, outside the walls. Small white stones cropped through the grass, over which low olive trees were scattered. The afternoon had a yellow brightness. I sat down under one of the little trees, on the grass – the delicate gray branches were not much above my head – and rested, and looked at Avignon across the Rhone. It was very soft, very still and pleasant, though I am not sure it was all I once should have expected of that combination of elements: an old city wall for a background, a canopy of olives, and, for a couch, the soil of Provence.

When I came back to Avignon the twilight was already thick; but I walked up to the Rocher des Doms. Here I again had the benefit of that amiable moon which had already lighted up for me so many romantic scenes. She was full, and she rose over the Rhone, and made it look in the distance like a silver serpent. I remember saying to myself at this moment, that it would be a beautiful evening to walk round the walls of Avignon, the remarkable walls, which challenge comparison with those of Carcassonne and Aigues-Mortes, and which it was my duty, as an observer of the picturesque, to examine with some attention. Presenting themselves to that silver sheen, they could not fail to be impressive. So, at least, I said to myself; but, unfortunately, I did not believe what I said. It is a melancholy fact that the walls of Avignon had never impressed me at all, and I had never taken the trouble to make the circuit. They are continuous and complete, but for some mysterious reason they fail of their effect. This is partly because they are very low, in some places almost absurdly so; being buried in new accumulations of soil, and by the filling in of the moat up to their middle. Then they have been too well tended; they not only look at present very new, but look as if they had never been old. The fact that their extent is very much greater makes them more of a curiosity than those of Carcassonne; but this is exactly, as the same time, what is fatal to their pictorial unity. With their thirty-seven towers and seven gates they lose themselves too much to make a picture that will compare with the admirable little vignette of Carcassonne. I may mention, now that I am speaking of the general mass of Avignon, that nothing is more curious than the way in which, viewed from a distance, it is all reduced to nought by the vast bulk of the palace of the Popes. From across the Rhone, or from the train, as you leave the place, this great gray block is all Avignon; it seems to occupy the whole city, extensive, with its shrunken population, as the city is.

XII

It was the morning after this, I think (a certain Saturday), that when I came out of the Hôtel de l'Europe, which lies in a shallow concavity just within the city gate that opens on the Rhone – came out to look at the sky from the little *place* before the inn, and see how the weather promised for the obligatory excursion to Vaucluse – I found the whole town in a terrible taking. I say the whole town advisedly; for every inhabitant appeared to have taken up a position on the bank of the river, or on the uppermost parts of the promenade of the Doms, where a view of its course was to be obtained. It had risen surprisingly in the night, and the good people of Avignon had reason to know what a rise of the Rhone might signify. The town, in its lower portions, is quite at the mercy of the swollen waters; and it was mentioned to me that in 1856 the Hôtel de l'Europe, in its convenient hollow, was flooded up to within a few feet of the ceiling of the dining room, where the long board which had served for so many a table d'hôte floated disreputably, with its legs in the air. On the present occasion the mountains of the Ardèche, where it had been raining for a month, had sent down torrents which, all that fine Friday night, by the light of the innocent-looking moon, poured themselves into the Rhone and its tributary, the Durance. The river was enormous, and continued to rise; and the sight was beautiful and horrible. The water in many places was already at the base of the city walls; the quay, with its parapet just emerging, being already covered. The country, seen from the Plateau des Doms, resembled a vast lake, with protrusions of trees, houses, bridges, gates. The people looked at it in silence, as I had seen people before – on the occasion of a rise of the Arno, at Pisa – appear to consider the prospects of an inundation. 'Il monte; il monte toujours,' – there was not much said but that. It was a general holiday, and there was an air of wishing to profit, for sociability's sake, by any interruption of the commonplace (the popular mind likes 'a change', and the element of change mitigates the sense of disaster); but the affair was not otherwise a holiday. Suspense and anxiety were in the air, and it never is pleasant to be reminded of the helplessness of man. In the presence of a loosened river, with its ravaging, unconquerable volume, this impression is as strong as possible; and as I looked at the deluge which threatened to make an island of the papal palace, I perceived that the scourge of water is greater than the scourge of fire. A blaze may be quenched, but where could the flame be kindled that would arrest the quadrupled Rhone? For the population of Avignon a good deal was at stake, and I am almost ashamed to confess that in the midst of the public alarm I considered the situation from the point of view of the little projects of a sentimental tourist. Would the prospective inundation interfere with my visit to Vaucluse, or make it imprudent to linger twenty-four hours longer at Avignon? I must add that the tourist was not perhaps, after all, so sentimental. I have spoken of the pilgrimage to the shrine of Petrarch as obligatory, and that was, in fact, the light in which it presented itself to me; all the more that I had been twice at Avignon without undertaking it. This is why I was vexed at the Rhone – if vexed I was – for representing as impracticable an excursion which I cared nothing about. How little I cared was manifest from my inaction on former occasions. I had a prejudice against Vaucluse, against Petrarch, even against the incomparable Laura. I was sure that the place was cockneyfied and threadbare, and I had never been able to take an interest in the poet and the lady. I was sure that I had known many women as charming and as handsome as she, about whom much less noise had been made; and I was convinced that her singer was factitious and literary, and that there are half a dozen stanzas in Wordsworth that speak more to the soul than the whole collection of his *fioriture*. This was the crude state of mind in which I determined to go, at any risk, to Vaucluse. Now that I think it over, I seem to remember that I had hoped, after all, that the submersion of the roads would forbid it. Since morning the clouds had gathered again, and by noon they were so heavy that there was every prospect of a torrent. It appeared absurd to choose such a time as this to visit a fountain – a fountain which would be indistinguishable in the general cataract. Nevertheless I took a vow that if at noon the rain should not have begun to descend upon Avignon I would repair to the head-spring of the Sorgues. When the critical moment arrived, the clouds were hanging over Avignon like distended water-bags, which only needed a prick to empty themselves. The prick was not given, however; all nature was too much occupied in following the aberration of the Rhone to think of playing tricks elsewhere. Accordingly, I started for the station in a spirit which, for a tourist who sometimes had prided himself on his unfailing supply of sentiment, was shockingly perfunctory.

> *For tasks in hours of insight willed*
> *May be in hours of gloom fulfilled.*

I remembered these lines of Matthew Arnold (written, apparently, in an hour of gloom), and carried out the idea, as I went, by hoping that with the return of insight I should be glad to have seen Vaucluse. Light has descended upon me since then, and I declare that the excursion is in every way to be recommended. The place makes a great impression, quite apart from Petrarch and Laura.

There was no rain; there was only, all the afternoon, a mild, moist wind, and a sky magnificently black, which made a *repoussoir* for the paler cliffs of the fountain. The road, by train, crosses a flat, expressionless country, toward the range of arid hills which lie to the east of Avignon, and which spring (says Murray) from the mass of the Mont-Ventoux. At Isle-sur-Sorgues, at the end of about an hour, the foreground becomes much more animated and the distance much more (or perhaps I should say much less) actual. I descended from the train, and ascended to the top of an omnibus which was to convey me into the recesses of the hills. It had not been among my pre-visions that I should be indebted to a vehicle of that kind for an opportunity to commune with the spirit of Petrarch; and I had to borrow what consolation I could from the fact that at least I had the omnibus to myself. I was the only passenger; everyone else was at Avignon, watching the Rhone. I lost no time in perceiving that I could not have come to Vaucluse at a better moment. The Sorgues was almost as full as the Rhone, and of a color much more romantic. Rushing along its narrowed channel under an avenue of fine *platanes* (it is confined between solid little embankments of stone), with the good-wives of the village, on the brink, washing their linen in its contemptuous flood, it gave promise of high entertainment further on.

The drive to Vaucluse is of about three quarters of an hour; and though the river, as I say, was promising, the big pale hills, as the road winds into them, did not look as if their slopes of stone and shrub were a nestling place for superior scenery. It is a part of the merit of Vaucluse, indeed, that it is as much as possible a surprise. The place has a right to its name, for the valley appears impenetrable until you get fairly into it. One perverse twist follows another, until the omnibus suddenly deposits you in front of the 'cabinet' of Petrarch. After that you have only to walk along the left bank of the river. The cabinet of Petrarch is today a hideous little *cafe*, bedizened, like a sign-board, with extracts from the ingenious 'Rime'. The poet and his lady are, of course, the stock in trade of the little village, which has had for several generations the privilege of attracting young couples engaged in their wedding tour, and other votaries of the tender passion. The place has long been familiar, on festal Sundays, to the swains of Avignon and their attendant nymphs. The little fish of the Sorgues are much esteemed, and, eaten on the spot, they constitute, for the children of the once papal city, the classic suburban dinner. Vaucluse has been turned to account, however, not only by sentiment, but by industry; the banks of the stream being disfigured by a pair of hideous mills for the manufacture of paper and of wool. In an enterprising and economical age the water-power of the Sorgues was too obvious a motive; and I must say that, as the torrent rushed past them, the wheels of the dirty little factories appeared to turn merrily enough. The footpath on the left bank, of which I just spoke, carries one, fortunately, quite out of sight of them, and out of sound as well, inasmuch as on the day of my visit the stream itself, which was in tremendous force, tended more and more, as one approached the fountain, to fill the valley with its own echoes. Its color was magnificent, and the whole spectacle more like a corner of Switzerland than a nook in Provence. The protrusions of the mountain shut it in, and you penetrate to the bottom of the recess which they form. The Sorgues rushes and rushes; it is almost like Niagara after the jump of the cataract. There are dreadful little booths beside the path, for the sale of photographs and *immortelles* – I don't know what one is to do with the *immortelles* – where you are offered a brush dipped in tar to write your name withal on the rocks. Thousands of vulgar persons, of both sexes, and exclusively, it appeared, of the French nationality, had availed themselves of this implement; for every square inch of accessible stone was scored over with some human appellation. It is not only we in America, therefore, who besmirch our scenery; the practice exists, in a more organized form (like everything else in France), in the country of good taste. You leave the little booths and stalls behind; but the bescribbled crag, bristling with human vanity, keeps you company even when you stand face to face with the fountain. This happens when you find yourself at the foot of the enormous straight cliff out of which the river gushes. It rears itself to an extraordinary height, a huge forehead of bare stone, looking as if it were the half of a tremendous mound, split open by volcanic action. The little valley, seeing it there, at a bend, stops suddenly, and receives in its arms the magical spring. I call it magical on account of the mysterious manner in which it comes into the world, with the huge shoulder of the mountain rising over it, as if to protect the secret. From under the mountain it silently rises, without visible movement, filling a small natural basin with the stillest blue water. The contrast between the stillness of this basin and the agitation of the water directly after it has overflowed, constitutes half the charm of Vaucluse. The violence of the stream when once it has been set loose on the rocks is as fascinating and indescribable as that of other cataracts; and the rocks in the bed of the Sorgues have been arranged by a master-hand. The setting of the phenomenon struck me as so simple and so fine – the vast sad cliff, covered with the afternoon light, still and solid forever, while the liquid element rages and roars at its base – that I had no difficulty in understanding the celebrity of Vaucluse. I understood it, but I will not say that I understood Petrarch. He must have been very self-supporting, and Madonna Laura must indeed have been much to him.

The aridity of the hills that shut in the valley is complete, and the whole impression is best conveyed by that very expressive French epithet *morne*. There are the very fragmentary ruins of a castle (of one of the bishops of Cavaillon) on a high spur of the mountain, above the river; and there is another remnant of a feudal habitation on one of the more accessible ledges. Having half an hour to spare before my omnibus was to leave (I must beg the reader's pardon for this atrociously false note; call the vehicle a *diligence*, and for some undiscoverable reason the offence is minimized), I clambered up to this latter spot, and sat among the rocks in the company of a few stunted olives. The Sorgues, beneath me, reaching the plain, flung itself crookedly across the meadows, like an unrolled blue ribbon. I tried to think of the *amant de Laure*, for literature's sake; but I had no great success, and the most I could do was to say to myself that I must try again. Several months have elapsed since then, and I am ashamed to confess that the trial has not yet come off. The only very definite conviction I arrived at was that Vaucluse is indeed cockneyfied, but that I should have been a fool, all the same, not to come.

XIII

I mounted into my *diligence* at the door of the Hôtel de Petrarque et de Laure, and we made our way back to Isle-sur-Sorgues in the fading light. This village, where at six o'clock everyone appeared to have gone to bed, was fairly darkened by its high, dense plane trees, under which the rushing river, on a level with its parapets, looked unnaturally, almost wickedly blue. It was a glimpse which has left a picture in my mind: the little closed houses, the place empty and soundless in the autumn dusk but for the noise of waters, and in the middle, amid the blackness of the shade, the gleam of the swift, strange tide. At the station everyone was talking of the inundation being in many places an accomplished fact, and, in particular, of the condition of the Durance at some point that I have forgotten. At Avignon, an hour later, I found the water in some of the streets. The sky cleared in the evening, the moon lighted up the submerged suburbs, and the population again collected in the high places to enjoy the spectacle. It exhibited a certain sameness, however, and by nine o'clock there was considerable animation in the Place Crillon, where there is nothing to be seen but the front of the theatre and of several cafes – in addition, indeed, to a statue of this celebrated brave, whose valor redeemed some of the numerous military disasters of the reign of Louis XV. The next morning the lower quarters of the town were in a pitiful state; the situation seemed to me odious. To express my disapproval of it, I lost no time in taking the train for Orange, which, with its other attractions, had the merit of not being seated on the Rhone. It was my destiny to move northward; but even if I had been at liberty to follow a less unnatural course I should not then have undertaken it, inasmuch as the railway between Avignon and Marseilles was credibly reported to be (in places) under water. This was the case with almost everything but the line itself, on the way to

Orange. The day proved splendid, and its brilliancy only lighted up the desolation. Farmhouses and cottages were up to their middle in the yellow liquidity; haystacks looked like dull little islands; windows and doors gaped open, without faces; and interruption and flight were represented in the scene. It was brought home to me that the *populations rurales* have many different ways of suffering, and my heart glowed with a grateful sense of cockneyism. It was under the influence of this emotion that I alighted at Orange, to visit a collection of eminently civil monuments.

The collection consists of but two objects, but these objects are so fine that I will let the word pass. One of them is a triumphal arch, supposedly of the period of Marcus Aurelius; the other is a fragment, magnificent in its ruin, of a Roman theatre. But for these fine Roman remains and for its name, Orange is a perfectly featureless little town; without the Rhone – which, as I have mentioned, is several miles distant – to help it to a physiognomy. It seems one of the oddest things that this obscure French borough – obscure, I mean, in our modern era, for the Gallo-Roman Arausio must have been, judging it by its arches and theatre, a place of some importance – should have given its name to the heirs apparent of the throne of Holland, and been borne by a king of England who had sovereign rights over it. During the Middle Ages it formed part of an independent principality; but in 1531 it fell, by the marriage of one of its princesses, who had inherited it, into the family of Nassau. I read in my indispensable Murray that it was made over to France by the treaty of Utrecht. The arch of triumph, which stands a little way out of the town, is rather a pretty than an imposing vestige of the Romans. If it had greater purity of style, one might say of it that it belonged to the same family of monuments as the Maison Carrée at Nîmes. It has three passages – the middle much higher than the others – and a very elevated attic. The vaults of the passages are richly sculptured, and the whole monument is covered with friezes and military trophies. This sculpture is rather mixed; much of it is broken and defaced, and the rest seemed to me ugly, though its workmanship is praised. The arch is at once well preserved and much injured. Its general mass is there, and as Roman monuments go it is remarkably perfect; but it has suffered, in patches, from the extremity of restoration. It is not, on the whole, of absorbing interest. It has a charm, nevertheless, which comes partly from its soft, bright yellow color, partly from a certain elegance of shape, of expression; and on that well washed Sunday morning, with its brilliant tone, surrounded by its circle of thin poplars, with the green country lying beyond it and a low blue horizon showing through its empty portals, it made, very sufficiently, a picture that hangs itself to one of the lateral hooks of the memory. I can take down the modest composition, and place it before me as I write. I see the shallow, shining puddles in the hard, fair French road; the pale blue sky, diluted by days of rain; the disgarnished autumnal fields; the mild sparkle of the low horizon; the solitary figure in sabots, with a bundle under its arm, advancing along the *chaussée*; and in the middle I see the little ochre-colored monument, which, in spite of its antiquity, looks bright and gay, as everything must look in France of a fresh Sunday morning.

It is true that this was not exactly the appearance of the Roman theatre, which lies on the other side of the town; a fact that did not prevent me from making my way to it in less than five minutes, through a succession of little streets concerning which I have no observations to record. None of the Roman remains in the south of France are more impressive than this stupendous fragment. An enormous mound rises above the place, which was formerly occupied – I quote from Murray – first by a citadel of the Romans, then by a castle of the princes of Nassau, razed by Louis XIV. Facing this hill a mighty wall erects itself, thirty-six metres high, and composed of massive blocks of dark brown stone, simply laid one on the other;

the whole naked, rugged surface of which suggests a natural cliff (say of the Vaucluse order) rather than an effort of human, or even of Roman labor. It is the biggest thing at Orange, it is bigger than all Orange put together and its permanent massiveness makes light of the shrunken city. The face it presents to the town – the top of it garnished with two rows of brackets, perforated with holes to receive the staves of the *velarium* – bears the traces of more than one tier of ornamental arches; though how these flat arches were applied, or incrusted, upon the wall, I do not profess to explain. You pass through a diminutive postern – which seems in proportion about as high as the entrance of a rabbit-hutch – into the lodge of the custodian, who introduces you to the interior of the theatre. Here the mass of the hill affronts you, which the ingenious Romans treated simply as the material of their auditorium. They inserted their stone seats, in a semicircle, in the slope of the hill, and planted their colossal wall opposite to it. This wall, from the inside, is, if possible, even more imposing. It formed the back of the stage, the permanent scene, and its enormous face was coated with marble. It contains three doors, the middle one being the highest, and having above it, far aloft, a deep niche, apparently intended for an imperial statue. A few of the benches remain on the hillside which, however, is mainly a confusion of fragments. There is part of a corridor built into the hill, high up, and on the crest are the remnants of the demolished castle. The whole place is a kind of wilderness of ruin; there are scarcely any details; the great feature is the overtopping wall. This wall being the back of the scene, the space left between it and the chord of the semicircle (of the auditorium) which formed the proscenium is rather less than one would have supposed. In other words, the stage was very shallow, and appears to have been arranged for a number of performers standing in a line, like a company of soldiers. There stands the silent skeleton, however, as impressive by what it leaves you to guess and wonder about as by what it tells you. It has not the sweetness, the softness of melancholy, of the theatre at Arles; but it is more extraordinary, and one can imagine only tremendous tragedies being enacted there –

Presenting Thebes' or Pelops' line.

At either end of the stage, coming forward, is an immense wing, immense in height, I mean, as it reaches to the top of the scenic wall; the other dimensions are not remarkable. The division to the right, as you face the stage, is pointed out as the green-room; its portentous attitude and the open arches at the top give it the air of a well. The compartment on the left is exactly similar, save that it opens into the traces of other chambers, said to be those of a hippodrome adjacent to the theatre. Various fragments are visible which refer themselves plausibly to such an establishment; the greater axis of the hippodrome would appear to have been on a line with the triumphal arch. This is all I saw, and all there was to see, of Orange, which had a very rustic, bucolic aspect, and where I was not even called upon to demand breakfast at the hotel. The entrance of this resort might have been that of a stable of the Roman days.

Biographical note

Henry James, novelist, playwright, short-story writer and critic, was born in New York in 1843. Educated in France, Germany and Switzerland, he attended Harvard Law School in 1862, later travelling extensively across Europe – an experience that inspired his first published books, two volumes of travel essays in 1875. His first published novel, *Roderick Hudson*, appeared the following year, depicting an American's moral decline in Rome, and relations between America and Europe formed the themes of further works, anticipating *The Portrait of a Lady* (1881).

From 1887, James lived in London, remaining there – his many European trips notwithstanding – until 1896, when he moved to Rye. His focus shifted to an exclusively English arena with his 1890 novel, *The Tragic Muse*, in which he explored the notion of the English character. He went on to pen biographies, literary criticism and the fragment of autobiography, *A Small Boy* and Others (1913), but in his later novels – *The Wings of the Dove* (1902), *The Ambassadors* (1903) and *The Golden Bowl* (1904) – he again returned to differences between America and Europe.

Today renowned as a master stylist whose novels often elaborate a moral consciousness torn between individual and social obligations, Henry James wrote with care and precision about Western civilisation as he understood it. Writing at a period when the novel form was reaching the heights of its sophistication, James critically examined the genre in his *The Art of Fiction* (1885), and praised Balzac above all other nineteenth-century novelists as 'the master of us all'. He assumed British nationality in 1915, dying the following year after suffering a stroke.